DAMN YANKEES

Random House
New York

Damn Yankees

A New Musical

(Based on the novel,
THE YEAR THE YANKEES
LOST THE PENNANT,
by Douglass Wallop)

Book by
GEORGE ABBOTT
and
DOUGLASS WALLOP

Music and Lyrics by
RICHARD ADLER
and
JERRY ROSS

Library of Congress Catalog Card Number: 56–6710

FIRST PRINTING

Photographs by Talbot

Damn Yankees *was presented first by Frederick Brisson,
Robert E. Griffith and Harold Prince, in association with Al-
bert B. Taylor, at the Forty-Sixth Street Theatre, New York
City, on May 5, 1955, with the following cast:*

(AS THEY APPEAR)

MEG	Shannon Bolin
JOE BOYD	Robert Shafer
APPLEGATE	Ray Walston
SISTER	Jean Stapleton
DORIS	Elizabeth Howell
JOE HARDY	Stephen Douglass
HENRY	Al Lanti
SOHOVIK	Eddie Phillips
SMOKEY	Nathaniel Frey
VERNON	Albert Linville
VAN BUREN	Russ Brown
ROCKY	Jimmy Komack
GLORIA	Rae Allen
TEEN-AGER	Cherry Davis
LYNCH	Del Horstmann
WELCH	Richard Bishop
LOLA	Gwen Verdon
MISS WESTON	Janie Janvier
COMMISSIONER	Del Horstmann
POSTMASTER	Albert Linville

DANCERS: Betty Carr, Margot Feldman, Patricia Ferrier, Mar-
lyn Greer, Marie Kolin, Julia Marlowe, Svetlana McLee,
Robert Evans, Timmy Everett, William Joyce, Harvey
Jung, Al Lanti, George Lake, Charles Morrell, Eddie
Phillips, Mark Ward.

SINGERS: Cherry Davis, Jeanne Grant, Janet Hayes, Janie Janvier, Joan Keenan, Suzanne Lovell, Frank Bouley, Fred Bryan, Del Horstmann, Ralph Lowe, Albert Linville, Ralph Strane.

CHILDREN: Ronn Cummins, Jackie Scholle.

Production directed by George Abbott

Dances and musical numbers staged by Bob Fosse

Scenery and costumes designed by William and Jean Eckart

Musical direction by Hal Hastings

Orchestrations by Don Walker

Dance music arrangements by Roger Adams

The action takes place some time in the future—

Washington, D.C.

MUSICAL NUMBERS

ACT ONE

Six Months Out of Every Year	Shannon Bolin, Robert Shafer, Baseball Fans, Baseball Widows
Goodbye, Old Girl	Robert Shafer, Stephen Douglass
Heart	Russ Brown, Jimmie Komack, Nathaniel Frey, Albert Linville
Shoeless Joe from Hannibal Mo.	Rae Allen and Baseball Players
A Man Doesn't Know	Stephen Douglass
A Little Brains—A Little Talent	Gwen Verdon
A Man Doesn't Know (Reprise)	Stephen Douglass, Shannon Bolin
Whatever Lola Wants	Gwen Verdon
Heart (Reprise)	Jean Stapleton, Ronn Cummins, Jackie Scholle, Cherry Davis
Who's Got the Pain?	Gwen Verdon and Eddie Phillips

(Dance staged by Bob Fosse and Gwen Verdon)

ACT TWO

The Game	Jimmie Komack, Nathaniel Frey and Baseball Players
Near to You	Stephen Douglass, Shannon Bolin
Those Were the Good Old Days	Ray Walston
Two Lost Souls	Gwen Verdon, Stephen Douglass and Guys and Dolls
A Man Doesn't Know (Reprise)	Shannon Bolin, Robert Shafer

ACT ONE

ACT ONE

SCENE I

The curtain is made of alternately colored strings of base-balls.

The curtain lifts, disclosing a typical suburban front porch and living room. JOE *is watching a ball game on television.* MEG *sits nearby sewing. It is a very warm evening. They are a comfortable couple in their forties.*

JOE

A strike—you're nuts. He's nuts.

MEG

Back home in Hannibal we had heat over 100 lots of times.

JOE

(Slides down in his chair)

Slide.

MEG

Casper Niles tried to fry an egg on the sidewalk in front of his drugstore one time.

JOE

Good old Smokey, he got a hit.

MEG

In Hannibal they were always saying cool air was on its

3

way from Canada. I certainly don't see any sign of it here, do you? (*No reply*) Do you?

JOE

Do I what?

MEG

See any sign of cool air . . . ?

JOE

You're blind, Ump. You're blind. See any sign of what, dear?

MEG

Never mind. (*Music begins*) It wasn't important. (*She continues to sew as she sings*)

When we met in nineteen thirty-eight, it was November
When I said that I would be his mate, it was December
I reasoned he would be the greatest husband that a girl
    had ever found
That's what I reasoned
That's what I reasoned
Then April rolled around.

JOE

(JOE *leans forward in his chair, begins to sing to the television set*)
Strike three, ball four, walk a run'll tie the score.
Yer blind, Ump,
Yer blind, Ump,
Ya mus' be out-a yer mind, Ump!

MEG

Six months out of every year

4

I might as well be made of stone
Six months out of every year when I'm with him
I'm alone.

JOE

He caught the corner.

MEG

Six months out of every year
He doesn't take me anywhere
Six months out of every year, when I play cards
Solitaire.
  (*She rises, walks to the screen door and leans against it*)
The other six months out of every year
We are hardly ever seen apart
But then the Washington Senators take over my place in
  his heart.
Six months out of every year
I might as well be wearing crepe
Life is just an awful bore from which I find no escape
Six months out of every year.
  (*A chorus of men from the neighborhood enters. All
  are wearing the same tie and slacks as* JOE. *They kneel
  downstage and sing.*)

BOYS

Strike three
Ball four
Walk a run'll tie the score
Fly ball
Double play
Yankees win again today.

5

Those damn Yankees
Why can't we beat 'em?
He's out, he's safe, he's out, he's safe, he's out, he's safe,
he's out.

> (*A chorus of neighborhood women, all in identical
> gaily colored aprons, enters. Takes the other side of
> stage*)

Yer blind Ump,
Yer blind Ump, you must be out of yer mind Ump.

GIRLS

> (*Now the stage is divided equally between the men and
> women and they sing against each other*)

Six months out of every year
He lives by the television set.

BOYS

He's out, he's safe, he's out!

GIRLS

If you see that man of mine
How does he look?
I forget.

BOYS

Le-e-ets go!

GIRLS

Six months out of every year
We know there is no other dame
If he isn't home by six,

BOYS

He's out, he's safe, he's out!

DAMN YANKEES

GIRLS

It's six to one
There's a game

BOYS

Le-e-ets go!

GIRLS

Six months out of every year when we cook for them it
never pays

BOYS

Aahh!

GIRLS

Instead of praising our goulash
They are appraising the plays of Willie Mays!

BOYS

He's out, he's safe, he's out!

GIRLS

Six months out of every year

BOYS

Strike three ball four walk a run'll tie the score

GIRLS

We might as well be wearing crepe

BOYS

Fly ball double play, Yankees win again today

GIRLS

Life is just an awful bore
From which there is no escape.

BOYS

Those damn Yankees. Why can't we beat em?
He's out, he's safe, he's out, he's safe, he's out, he's safe,
he's out.
Yer blind Ump, yer blind Ump
Ya must be out-a yer mind Ump.
(*Girls snake across the stage and line up in front of the men.*)

GIRLS

We're dying for the mercury to drop to three below

BOYS

Yay team

GIRLS

We're crying for the happy days of icicles and snow

BOYS

Yay team

GIRLS

We don't mind sleepin' solo, that is once a year or so,

BOYS

Those damn Yankees

GIRLS

But with them it's a career

8

BOYS

What are ya waitin' for?
April, May, June, July, August, September

GIRLS

April, May, June, July, August, September
Six months out of every year

BOYS

Yer blind Ump, yer blind Ump, ya must be out-a yer mind
Ump.
(*Neighbors exit in both directions and we see* MEG
standing by the screen door and JOE *watching television as before.*)

ALL

April, May, June, July, August, September.
April, May, June, July, August, September.

MEG

Six months out of every year.
(*Goes back to her chair and knitting.*)

JOE

Yer blind ump, yer blind ump, ya must be . . .
(*Speaks*)
O.K. Sohovik, don't try to murder it. . . . Just slip one
through the infield . . . Come on, Sohovik, get lucky . . .
Oh boy . . . (*To her*) The ball's in the dirt and he swings.
That does it!
(JOE *snaps off the television.*)

MEG

Did the Washington Senators win, dear? (*He grunts*) Oh,
I'm sorry. Well, maybe they will next time.

9

JOE

Damn Yankees.

MEG

What, dear?

JOE

I'd like to lick those damn Yankees just once.

MEG

But how can you if they're the champions?

JOE

If we had just one long ball hitter—just one—

MEG

Honestly, Joe, you're going to get yourself a stroke if you keep this up—or at least ulcers.

JOE

(Takes a swing at an imaginary ball)
Wham!

MEG

Oh, Joe, now my friends Sister and Doris—they like baseball but they don't suffer so. *(Rises)* Well, I'm going to bed. I've got the bridge club tomorrow. Good night.
(She kisses him. Exits upstairs.)

JOE

Yeah, sure—I mean good night. Good night, old girl. *(Goes out onto porch. Takes another swing at imaginary ball)* Wham! One long ball hitter, that's what we need. I'd sell my soul for one long ball hitter. (*There is eerie music.* JOE *looks up, as if conscious of some new element, steps off porch inquisitively. At this instant,* APPLEGATE *appears on the porch as if by magic. He is a slight man and dapper dresser*) Hey, where did you come from?

APPLEGATE

Good evening.

JOE

Who are you?

APPLEGATE

A man who agrees with you.

JOE

Agrees?

APPLEGATE

One long ball hitter—that's what the team needs.

JOE

You are right about that. You live around here?

APPLEGATE

My name is Applegate, and I think we have something in common, a love of the national game.

JOE

You bet. Care to sit down?
(*They both sit.* APPLEGATE *crosses his legs, showing a pair of bright red socks.*)

APPLEGATE

Thanks. You don't like to see the Senators in seventh place.

JOE

Well, they may pull together yet.

APPLEGATE

I'm here to make you a proposition. Not only would you like to see Washington win a pennant, but your secret yearning all your life has been to be a baseball player yourself.

JOE

I wasn't so bad in high school.

APPLEGATE

Not so bad! They were scouting you for Kansas City. You've still got your spike shoes and your glove—they're up in your bedroom.

JOE

Who told you?

APPLEGATE

Would you like to be the greatest baseball player in all history?

JOE

Big joke.

APPLEGATE

No joke. You can be a great ball player.

JOE

I can't even bend over and touch my toes.

DAMN YANKEES

 APPLEGATE

Try it. Just for laughs.
(JOE *shrugs and tries to bend over.* APPLEGATE *motions with his hand. Suddenly* JOE *can go down to his toes easily. He looks up surprised.*)

JOE

What do you know!

APPLEGATE

With my help a lot of things come easy. (*He makes a sudden move, there is a flash of fire and he is smoking a lighted cigarette*) Do you smoke?

JOE

Hey, how'd you pull that off?

APPLEGATE

I'm handy with fire.

JOE

Who are you?

APPLEGATE

I am quite a famous character, Mr. Boyd. I have historical significance too. In fact, I'm responsible for most of the history you can name.

JOE

Listen, I don't know what the gag is.
(*A pair of middle-aged friends of* MEG'S *enter,* SISTER *and* DORIS MILLER. *They affect youthful clothes and mannerisms and yammer a great deal. They ignore* APPLEGATE *as if they didn't see him.*)

13

SISTER

Talking to yourself! So you finally flapped your lid. What are you doing out here talking to yourself? In the dark?

JOE

(*Looking at* APPLEGATE)

Talking to who?

SISTER

It's a sign of old age, you know, Joe, talking to yourself.

JOE

It is?

SISTER

Is anything the matter?

JOE

I was just thinking about the game.

DORIS

(*Laughs*)

We went to the game yesterday—it was ladies' day.

SISTER

And I must say the hot dogs out at the park aren't what they used to be. I had the poorest hot dog yesterday I ever had.

DORIS

Is Meg still up?

JOE

No—she went to bed a while ago.

DORIS

We'll see her at bridge club tomorrow.
(*She exits.*)

SISTER

We just came from our ballet lesson.
(*Follows her sister off.*)

JOE

(*Incredulously*)
They couldn't see you.

APPLEGATE

No they couldn't—an amusing little stunt—it was all the
rage in the Middle Ages.

JOE

(*Stunned, he sits down on the edge of the porch*)
I think the heat's got me. You mean you really are?

APPLEGATE

Can't believe it, eh?

JOE

But that's crazy. It can't be.

APPLEGATE

The world is full of crazy things. Crazier every day.

JOE

Gosh. What are you doing here?

APPLEGATE

Great events bring forth great men, Joe. They arise from nowhere—they take command. That's history.

JOE

What are you talking about?

APPLEGATE

I have chosen you, the most dedicated partisan of the noble Washington Senators, to be the hero who leads them out of the wilderness to the championship.

JOE

The Senators are in seventh place.

APPLEGATE

Your powerful bludgeon and sparkling play will inspire the team to greatness. We'll call you Hardy—Joe Hardy. You will be twenty-two years old. They'll put a new wing on that baseball museum at Cooperstown, dedicated to you—the Hardy shrine.

JOE

Well—well—what do you want me to do?

APPLEGATE

Just leave everything to me.

JOE

My job—my wife.

APPLEGATE

This is a big operation. Can't let things like that stand in the way.

JOE

I just disappear, is that it?

APPLEGATE

Very simple.

JOE

And what happens after I stop being a baseball player? Then where would I be?

APPLEGATE

Well now, of course, that's fairly well known.

JOE

Yes, but—

APPLEGATE

After all there's nothing unusual about it. How do you suppose some of these politicians around town got started—and parking lot owners.

JOE

Still—If what they say—

APPLEGATE

Look, I've got something to trade here. I'm offering you a chance to be what you wanted to be all your life.

JOE

In my business we have what you call an escape clause.

APPLEGATE

This is not a real estate deal.

JOE

(*Stubbornly*)

If I don't like it, I ought to be able to get out.

APPLEGATE

Get out?

JOE

I've got my wife to consider.

APPLEGATE

(*Impatiently*)

All right, all right. I don't want to hear any more about your wife. Wives! They cause me more trouble than the Methodist Church. I'm trying to be understanding, but all this haggling. All right, I'll give you a chance to get out.

JOE

Well sure, in that case—

APPLEGATE

On the twenty-fourth of September at midnight. I wouldn't do it, but I don't want to have those damn Yankees win.

JOE

You can say that again.

APPLEGATE

(*They clasp hands*)

It's a deal.

JOE
(Surprised)

It is!

APPLEGATE

And now the other hand.

JOE
(Shaking hands left-handedly)

That's all?

APPLEGATE

Sure. What do you expect to do, sign your name in blood, or some phony stunt like that? Come on. The team needs you, let's not waste any more time.

JOE

I want to leave a note for my wife. (He goes into living room) And get my shoes and my glove.
(Exits upstairs.)

APPLEGATE

(Follows into living room, calls upstairs)
O.K., tell her you're going to Little America, to interest the Eskimos in split-level houses.
(Goes back onto porch.)

JOE

(Comes downstairs with glove and spike shoes)
I'm nearly ready.

APPLEGATE

I'll call a taxi.

(APPLEGATE *exits. Music starts.* JOE *picks up pad and
pencil on table and sits in chair. Sings while writing.*)
Goodbye, old girl,
My old girl,
When you awaken I'll be gone,
Can't tell you where I go,
It isn't fair, I know,
But trust in me and carry on.
Goodbye old friend,
My old friend,
There's somethin' I must let you know,
I haven't said it much,
I guess I've lost my touch,
But, my old girl, I love you so,
Now I know it hasn't all been rosy,
We've had squabblin' days when tears were brought about,
But in a moment or two we would bill and coo
And never even knew
What we fought about,
And now your Joe has to go,
But he'll come back to you again,
So sleep your sleep, old girl,
> (*Goes to the writing desk—finishes his note seated
> with his back to audience*)
Our love will keep, old girl, till then.
> (*The music swells for a few bars. The spotlight dims
> down and out as* APPLEGATE *enters on the porch.*
> APPLEGATE *crosses to screen door, looks in, smiles,
> pulls another lighted cigarette out of the air, takes a
> puff and, standing at the porch door, makes magical
> pass in the direction of* JOE BOYD. *He opens door to the
> house and surveys his work for a second.*)

APPLEGATE

All right, cab's waiting.

JOE

(*Rises. He is a different man—twenty years younger, lean and athletic. His clothes are much too big for him. For the second he only senses the change*)

Hey. Did you? (*Pulls in pants which are much too large for him*) I can't believe it. (*Takes batting stance and swings at imaginary ball*) Wham!

(*Picks up shoes and glove. Throws back his head and sings exultantly in his powerful young voice*)

And though your Joe has to go,
He may come back to you again,
So sleep your sleep old girl,
Our love will keep old girl, till then,
Goodbye old girl.

APPLEGATE

Come on.

(*Goes out onto porch and exits.* JOE *follows.*)

JOE

My old girl
Goodbye.

(JOE *runs off after* APPLEGATE.)

SCENE II

A corridor under the stands of the Washington Baseball Park. An arrow in the tile wall points in one direction to the stands. Two ball players dressed in uniforms are talking.

HENRY

Do you have to sell insurance in the summer too?

SOHOVIK

I don't have to but when I see a guy like you that's not covered, I get worried.

HENRY

I've been uncovered a long time. I don't worry.

SOHOVIK

Everybody should have an insurance program.
(SMOKEY, *a thick-set, slow-witted fellow enters, carrying a crossword puzzle.*)

HENRY

Next year maybe. How's the crossword coming, Smokey?

SMOKEY

Very difficult.
(HENRY *looks over* SMOKEY's *shoulder. Two players enter.*)

VERNON

So Ferguson give me the signal to steal, it was a pitch-out and when I got to second, everybody was waiting for me except Ford Frick.

SMOKEY

Hey, Sohovik, what's a three-letter word for a sticky substance? (SOHOVIK *points in his mouth, where he is chewing gum*) Spit? No, that's four.

SOHOVIK

Gum.

(BENNY VAN BUREN, *the wiry white-haired manager of the team enters with* ROCKY, *who is as good-natured as they come.*)

SMOKEY

Gum!

VAN BUREN

Look—Rocky—What sign is this?
(*Goes through routine of complicated signals.*)

ROCKY

Hit and run, sure.

VAN BUREN

Right. Now you're still at bat.
(ROCKY *takes stance.* VAN BUREN *signals again.*)

ROCKY

I take.

VAN BUREN

O.K. Now the count's two and one.
(*He signals.*)

23

ROCKY

I don't do nothin'.

VAN BUREN

How can you not do nothing? If I wipe the take signal watch what follows. (*He signals.* ROCKY *looks dumfounded*) You go for it.

ROCKY

Oh, sure.

VAN BUREN

Why couldn't you remember that last night, you could have cost us a big inning?

ROCKY

It's not that I'm dumb, Benny.

VAN BUREN

Nobody said anything about your being dumb, exactly.

ROCKY

It's just that when we play the Yankees I kind of tense up. I kind of lose my head. I figure what the hell is the use.

VAN BUREN

Will you listen to this guy?

SMOKEY

Benny, there is something different about 'em.

VAN BUREN

What do you mean?

ROCKY

Well, we don't make them same goofers when we're playing Kansas City.

VAN BUREN

Now, listen, all of you, that's what I'm talking about. Boys,
I know you're not yellow. Smokey, you bang into fences until you drive me crazy, and Rocky, you played three games
with a broken hand. But your mental state is all off in left
field. Now listen to me: Baseball is only one half skill—the
other half is something else. Something bigger. (*He sings*)

You've gotta have heart
All you really need is heart
When the odds are sayin' you'll never win,
That's when the grin should start.
You've gotta have hope
Mustn't sit around and mope
Nothin's half as bad as it may appear
Wait'll next year and hope.
When your luck is battin' zero
Get your chin up off the floor;
Mister you can be a hero
You can open any door, there's nothin' to it, but to do it.
You've gotta have heart
Miles 'n miles 'n miles of heart
Oh, it's fine to be a genius of course
But keep that old horse
Before the cart
First you've gotta have heart.
    (*The boys get the idea—start to sing.*)

ROCKY

(*Looking at* SMOKEY)

A great slugger we haven't got

SMOKEY

(*Looking at* VERNON)

A great pitcher we haven't got

VERNON

A great ball club we haven't got

ROCKY, SMOKEY, AND VERNON

(*All look at* BENNY)

What've we got?

ALL

We've got heart
All you really need is heart
When the odds are sayin' you'll never win,
That's when the grin should start.

VAN BUREN

(*Speaks*)

Now you're getting the idea.

ROCKY, SMOKEY AND LINVILLE

(*Sing*)

We've got hope
We don't sit around and mope
Not a solitary sob do we heave
Mister, 'cause we've got hope.

VAN BUREN

(*Speaks*)

Boys, I'm proud of you.

26

ROCKY

(*Sings*)

We're so happy that we're hummin'

ALL

(*Unenthusiastically*)

Hmm—hmm—hmm

VAN BUREN

That's the hearty thing to do

ALL

Hoo—hoo—hoo

SMOKEY

'Cause we know our ship will come in

ALL

Hmm—hmm—hmm

(*They don't believe this either.*)

ROCKY

So it's ten years overdue

ALL

Hoo—hoo—hoo

We've got heart

Miles 'n miles 'n miles o' heart

VERNON

Oh, it's fine to be a genius of course

BOYS

But keep that old horse before the cart.

VAN BUREN

So what the heck's the use of cryin'?

SMOKEY

Why should we curse?

ROCKY

We've gotta get better 'cause we can't get worse!

ALL

And to add to it, we've got heart,
We've got heart
We've got heart!
> (*On applause,* SMOKEY, VERNON *and* ROCKY *start out,*
> GLORIA *enters. She is the prototype of the professional
> woman—not bad-looking if you ignore the fierce com-
> petitive manner.*)

VAN BUREN

Wait a minute—tell it to her.
> (SMOKEY, VERNON *and* ROCKY *come back and sing.*)

ALL

We've got heart
All you really need is heart
When the odds are sayin' you'll never win
That's when the grin should start.

SMOKEY

We're so happy that we're laughin'

ALL

Ha ha ha

VAN BUREN

That's the hearty thing to do

ALL

Hoo, hoo, hoo,

VERNON

So we ain't been autographin'

ALL

Ha ha ha

ROCKY

'Cept to sign an I.O.U.

ALL

Hoo hoo hoo
(*Crying—their shoulders sag.*)

ALL

We've got heart,
Miles 'n miles 'n miles of heart
Oh, it's fine to be a genius of course
But keep that old horse before the cart

SMOKEY

Who minds those pop bottles flyin'

VERNON

The hisses and boos

VAN BUREN

The team has been consistent

ROCKY

Yeah, we always lose

THREE BOYS

But we're laughin' cause . . . we've got *heart*

ALL FOUR

We've got heart . . . we've got heart.
(*They exit.*)

GLORIA

Well, I've often wondered what this team did to keep up its morale.

VAN BUREN

We didn't invite the press this morning, Gloria.

GLORIA

Benny, you're very foolish to have this prejudice against me just because I'm a woman. My paper gives you as much space as the others do.

VAN BUREN

I only wondered why you were here so early.

GLORIA

I came down to see the naked men.

VAN BUREN

Could be.

GLORIA

My boss is very anxious to find out what some of your players think of the Yankees.

DAMN YANKEES

VAN BUREN

I'll tell you something right now—my players don't play dead for the Yankees or any other club.

(APPLEGATE *enters during the last part of this speech followed by* JOE *in a new suit carrying his glove and spiked shoes.*)

APPLEGATE

Are you Mr. Van Buren, the Washington manager?

VAN BUREN

(*Ignoring* APPLEGATE *he turns back to* GLORIA)
Why make something out of the Yankees? They're a swell bunch of fellas and . . .

GLORIA

Oh yes, they're very polite and then they beat your brains out.

VAN BUREN

They're just another team as far as we're concerned.

APPLEGATE

I read somewhere that they're talking about handicapping the Yankees—making them carry extra weight like with horses.

VAN BUREN

Yeah? So what the hell's on your mind, Mac?

APPLEGATE

Applegate is my name. (*Produces card from the air*) My card, sir.

VAN BUREN

I'm busy, see my secretary.

APPLEGATE

Mr. Van Buren, I'm a long-time fan of the Washington Senators.

VAN BUREN

Listen, Mac, I told you I'm busy.

APPLEGATE

And for some time now I've been beating the bushes for talent. This is my protégé, young Joe Hardy. Joe's quite a boy with a bat in his hands and I'd like you to give him a trial.

VAN BUREN

Where have you been playing, son?

JOE

Oh, here and there.

VAN BUREN

Where's here and there?

JOE

If you just let me hit a few, Mr. Van Buren.

APPLEGATE

What have you got to lose?

VAN BUREN

(*Calling off toward the dugout*)

Smokey.

APPLEGATE

He can hit the ball a country mile.

SMOKEY

(*Enter, carrying crossword book*)
You call me, Benny?

VAN BUREN

I want you to take this kid down to the locker room.

JOE

Gee, thanks Mr. Van Buren. And I certainly hope—

VAN BUREN

(*Cutting him off*)
Tell Buster to throw him a few.

SMOKEY

Sure thing. Come on, Mac.
(SMOKEY *and* JOE *exit.* APPLEGATE *starts to follow them, but is stopped by* VAN BUREN.)

VAN BUREN

Hey, wait a minute. Where do you think you're going?

APPLEGATE

My protégé may need my advice.

VAN BUREN

Buster will give him all the advice he needs. If you want to look, go out in the stands. The field is for ball players. You don't mind do you?

33

APPLEGATE

Love it, Mac, just love it. (VAN BUREN *exits to the dugout.* APPLEGATE *turns to* GLORIA) Are you coming, my attractive friend?

GLORIA

Well, I'll look, but nothing will happen.

APPLEGATE

Want to bet?
(APPLEGATE *and* GLORIA *exit to the stands.*)

(*Blackout*)

Scene III

In the dark there is the crack of a ball being hit by a bat offstage. Crack. The lights come up on the dugout of the Washington Baseball Park. Behind the dugout stretch the boxes and then the empty stands, and in the distance a strip of blue sky behind the last row of seats.

van buren and several players sit on the step of the dugout or stand leaning against the rail. All are looking out. They then look diagonally off left where the batters' box is. They chew gum. There is another crack and all heads turn as they follow the imaginary ball in flight. After the ball has landed they all resume chewing gum violently till the next crack is heard, and the business is repeated once more.

VAN BUREN

I can't believe the kid is as good as all that. How could he be—where the hell would he have been keeping himself? Henry.

HENRY

Yes, Benny.

VAN BUREN

Go out there and tell Buster to throw hard.

HENRY

He is throwing hard, can't you hear him grunt?

VAN BUREN

Well, go out there and tell him to bear down.

35

HENRY

Sure.

(*He trots off.*)

ROCKY

Batting practice is one thing—but how does he do in a game, eh?

SOHOVIK

He's got a nice swing.

(*Crack. They all look till the ball arcs far away.*)

SMOKEY

She's gone.

SOHOVIK

Over the fence.

ROCKY

It's just luck.

VAN BUREN

This is costing the club money. (*He calls off*) Hey, kid. Yeah—you—come here.

SOHOVIK

That boy has a career ahead of him, and I bet he hasn't a dime's worth of insurance.

(JOE *enters.* VAN BUREN *turns to him.*)

VAN BUREN

What'd they say your name was? Joe?

JOE

Yes, sir. Joe. Joe Hardy.

VAN BUREN

You hit the ball pretty good.

JOE

Thanks.

VAN BUREN

How's your fielding?

JOE

I don't know?

VAN BUREN

You don't know?

JOE

I mean my manager was supposed to be here—he—ah—
(*He turns and looks helplessly.*)

APPLEGATE

(*Enters in the stands, comes down to the boxes above the dugout*)
Did you want me, Joe?

JOE

Yes, Mr. Applegate, I—they want me to field some.

APPLEGATE

Well, go ahead boy, you can do anything—you know that.

VAN BUREN

What position do you play?

JOE

I'd like to be a shortstop.

VAN BUREN

Okay, get out there.
(JOE *exits to the field.*)

37

APPLEGATE

How you like my boy, Mr. Van Buren?

VAN BUREN

Not bad.

APPLEGATE

Not bad! Did he kiss that horsehide right out of the park—
did he get the fat end of the bat on that pill. Bye-bye baby.
How about that.

ROCKY

Who's up there? Mel Allen?
  (*Crack of bat.*)

APPLEGATE

           (*Yelling out to* JOE)

Dig, boy, dig.

VAN BUREN

Say—he's got an arm.

APPLEGATE

Got an arm—he's got an arm like a cannon.

VAN BUREN

Hit a couple of Texas leaguers. Let's see how he moves
back under 'em.
      (*Crack of bat. During this* GLORIA *has entered in the
      grandstand and now sits a seat away from* APPLEGATE.)

GLORIA

What's the story on this kid?

APPLEGATE

You saw where he was hitting 'em, didn't you? Over the garden wall. (*Crack of bat*) Attaboy, Joe, rifle it home, boy, rifle it home.

GLORIA

Where'd he come from?

APPLEGATE

His name is Joe Hardy.

VAN BUREN
(*Calling off*)

O.K., Joe, come on in.

GLORIA

Who's he been playing for?

APPLEGATE
(*Ignoring her*)

He weighs 193 pounds, chews Juicy Fruit.

GLORIA

You're a big help.
(JOE *enters.*)

VAN BUREN

Never played anything but sandlot ball, huh? Whereabouts?
(JOE *stammers unsurely.*)

APPLEGATE

Out West.

JOE

The Midwest. Oh! Hannibal. Hannibal, Missouri.
(HENRY *helps* GLORIA *down onto the field from the stands.*)

GLORIA

Is that your home town?

JOE

Yeah—yeah, that's it. Boy, does it get hot there sometimes!
We just sit around and wait for the cold air to come down
from Canada.

VAN BUREN

You do all right.

JOE

Thanks.

VAN BUREN

I think we might give you a contract, send you to one of
our farm clubs for a little seasoning.
(GLORIA *takes notebook out and is about to write.*)

APPLEGATE

(*Impatiently leaving the stands*)
Seasoning? That's ridiculous.

VAN BUREN

How about it, kid?

JOE

No sir, I don't think so.

VAN BUREN

What do you mean?

JOE

I haven't got time.

VAN BUREN

Time?

APPLEGATE

Baseball's in a rut. If Ty Cobb came here looking for a chance you'd send him to Little Rock. All right, Joe, come on we'll go where we'll be appreciated.

JOE

Gee, Mr. Van Buren, give me one more chance, will you? I love the Senators.

GLORIA

So do I and there's only a few of us left.

VAN BUREN

Get your bat. (JOE *runs off.* VAN BUREN *calls off to the pitcher*) Buster.
> (*He gestures—"give him your toughest." All watch intently. There is a loud crack. All the players jump up and come downstage.*)

APPLEGATE

More seasoning, eh? The ball's only going for a 600-foot ride.

VAN BUREN

That's the longest ball I ever saw in my life.

ROCKY

(*Gulps*)
I swallowed my chewin' tobacco.

VAN BUREN

I just can't believe it—where could he have been all these years? (JOE *enters*) O.K. You win. Get a uniform.

JOE

(*Stunned*)

You mean it?

VAN BUREN

Yes, I mean it.

JOE

(*Wildly enthusiastic*)

Yow! I made it. (JOE *rushes to* APPLEGATE *who is still in the stands, pumps his hand*) You were right. Oh, man oh man! Mr. Applegate, how can I ever thank you?

APPLEGATE

I'll find some way.

JOE

Oh baby, this is wonderful. (*He grabs* SMOKEY *around the waist, jumps up and down. Then sits down to take off his shoes*) Listen, you guys, don't think I'm crazy, or going off my chump or something. But you got no idea what this means.
(APPLEGATE *climbs down from stands to field.*)

SOHOVIK

Feels good, eh, Joe?

JOE

All my life I dreamed—oh gee.
(*He starts to untie shoelaces.*)

42

VAN BUREN

(Pats JOE's *shoulder)*

Just take it easy, kid.

JOE

I will, I will.
(Still fumbling.)

VAN BUREN

I don't want you to get so excited you'll tense up on us.

JOE

I must have tied the wrong knot.

SOHOVIK

Let me wait on you, boy. I got a hunch you're going to bring us luck.

*(*SOHOVIK *kneels down and begins to untie* JOE's *right shoe.)*

ROCKY

Me too.
(Starts loosening other shoe.)

JOE
(Protesting)

Oh, no.

ROCKY

Sit still.

GLORIA
(To VAN BUREN*)*

Well, I'm glad I came by this morning.

43

APPLEGATE

(*Out of stands*)
Something happened after all, eh?

GLORIA

(*To* APPLEGATE)
Give me the real story on this, will you?

APPLEGATE

He's a natural talent—that's all.

GLORIA

Oh, don't be coy—

JOE

Thanks very much for the loan of your shoes.

VERNON

You did right by them, Joe.

GLORIA

What was the matter with your own shoes? I saw you bringing in a pair.

JOE

Those were too small for me.

GLORIA

Your own shoes?

JOE

Yeah. I guess my feet had swollen. Maybe it was the excitement or the heat or something.

DAMN YANKEES

VAN BUREN

Come on, Joe, I'll take you up to the office. I'll have you meet Mr. Welch.

(VAN BUREN—*followed by* JOE *and* APPLEGATE.)

JOE

Oh great! Shouldn't I put on my shoes?
(*They exit.*)

GLORIA

(*Writing in notebook*)
I've got it—Shoeless Joe Hardy.

SMOKEY

That's what you're going to call him?

GLORIA

That's what everybody is going to call him. I'll give this club some publicity.

SOHOVIK

Shoeless Joe, huh! Pretty good.

GLORIA

I'll help you celebrate, boys.

VERNON

What's the gag?

GLORIA

Let's make Joe famous.

SMOKEY

Sure—I'm willing.

ROCKY

O.K., how do we make him famous?
(*Three of the boys whistle a tune and* GLORIA *sings.*)

GLORIA

Shoeless Joe from Hannibal Mo.
(*The tune is repeated*)

BOYS

Shoeless Joe from Hannibal Mo.

SOHOVIK

(*Speaks*)
A little hoe down in honor of our new star.

ALL

(*Sing*)
Shoeless Joe from Hannibal Mo.

MARK

(*Speaks*)
What'd she say his name was?

ALL

Shoeless Joe from Hannibal Mo.
(*They clap their hands and start to dance and the
orchestra comes in.*)

SMOKEY

(*Speaks over the music*)
She's gonna call him Shoeless Joe. Gee, Miss Thorpe, you
sure get some wonderful ideas.

GLORIA

(*Speaks*)

Oh, I got lots of ideas.
    (*Sings*)
Who came along in a puff of smoke?

ALL

Shoeless Joe from Hannibal Mo.

GLORIA

Strong as the heart of the mighty oak

ALL

Shoeless Joe from Hannibal Mo.
Lucky are we to be having him.

GLORIA

Shoeless Joe from Hannibal Mo.

ALL

Just when the future was lookin' grim

GLORIA

Shoeless Joe from Hannibal Mo.

ALL

Came a long long way to be
With us today

GLORIA

With arms of steel like Hercules

BOYS

Yeow!

GLORIA

Feet as fleet as Mercury's

BOYS

Yeah!

GLORIA

He'll fight
For us, do right for us

ALL

He'll be a beacon light for us
He's Shoeless Joe from Hannibal Mo.
Go, go, go, go, go, go,

GLORIA

Go like a bat out-a you know where,

ALL

Shoeless Joe from Hannibal Mo!

GLORIA

Strike at the foe, let 'em know you're there,

ALL

Shoeless Joe from Hannibal Mo!
Shoeless Joe from Hannibal Mo!
Shoeless Joe from Hannibal Mo!

GLORIA

Came upon the scene

ALL

As fresh as Listerine,

48

GLORIA

He sneezed and blew away a calf
His laughter ripped a barn in half

ALL

Go, go, go, go, Joe

GLORIA

Like sevens come, elevens come,

ALL

Like manna from the heavens come!
It's Shoeless Joe from Hannibal Mo.
Go, go, go, go, go, go, go, go
Go like a bat out-a you know where,

GLORIA

Shoeless Joe from M.O.
Strike at the foe
Let 'em know you're there,

ALL

Shoeless Joe from M.O.
Look out, look out, look out, look out for Shoeless Joe

JOE

The barefoot boy
From Hannibal Mo!

BOYS

Joe, Joe, Joe, Joe, Joe, Joe, Joe, Joe!
   (*They go into a dance, which illustrates all the famil-
   iar baseball attitudes.*)

(*Blackout*)

49

SCENE IV

A billboard near the ballpark. It is a picture of JOE *advertising some toothpaste. Three teen-agers, carrying autograph books are talking.*

FIRST TEEN-AGER

Joe Hardy is going to be interviewed by the press.

SECOND TEEN-AGER
(Looking off)

Here's one of the players.
(They run off in the direction of the player. SISTER *and* DORIS *run on from the other side—both carry autograph books.)*

DORIS
(Stops, realizing that SISTER *has stopped)*

Aren't you coming?

SISTER

No, I don't want him. I thought it was Joe Hardy.

DORIS

You'll never get Joe Hardy, they don't let you near him. Look out, here comes Mr. Welch.

SISTER

Who?

DORIS

Welch. The gentleman who owns the club.
(WELCH *enters followed by newspaper reporters. They cross.*)

LYNCH

Our readers are really burning to get some more dope on him.

WELCH

Of course they are, and we want to co-operate, in every way. That's why I asked you here. But you know sometimes I don't understand you boys.

SISTER

(*Walks up to* WELCH)

May I have your autograph, please? (WELCH *looks non-plused,* SISTER *smiles*) It's for my niece—she's sick—muscular diathermy.
(WELCH *signs absent-mindedly, continues walking.*)

WELCH

After all these lean years we bring you a truly great ball player. A man for you all to be proud of and right away this Gloria Thorpe starts sniping at him.

LYNCH

You know Gloria, Mr. Welch, the eager type, she's just curious.

WELCH

It doesn't help.

LYNCH

As a matter of fact, I'm curious myself. How about those shoes? How come he couldn't get into his own shoes?

WELCH

A pair of spiked shoes—they all look alike. He just picked up the wrong shoes, that's all. What's the mystery there? Good grief, this boy has gone from pinch hitter to idol of the nation in one month. He's making the whole team come to life. . . . (*They exit—the rest of the speech is heard from off-stage*) And then you fellows want to make trouble . . .

SISTER

And I'll get Joe Hardy's too.

FIRST TEEN-AGER

(*Re-enters, sees* APPLEGATE *who enters with press card in hat band*)

Here comes somebody.
　　(APPLEGATE *crosses briskly.*)

SISTER

He's nobody.

FIRST TEEN-AGER

Are you anybody?

APPLEGATE

Not a soul.

(*Blackout*)

Scene V

WELCH's *office, musty, oak-paneled backroom with baseball pictures, trophies, etc.*

JOE *enters followed by* VAN BUREN. JOE *is in an angry mood.*

VAN BUREN
Now, Joe. You mustn't be temperamental.

JOE
I'm not. Only the questions that Gloria Thorpe dame asks are none of her business.
(APPLEGATE *enters.*)

VAN BUREN
A good press means a lot to the front office, Joe. Come on, boy. Play ball with them a little, will you?

JOE
They're a bunch of crooks. You tell them one thing and they write down whatever comes into their heads.

VAN BUREN
(*To* APPLEGATE)
Look, you talk to him. I'll go in and say he's off his feed.
(VAN BUREN *exits.*)

APPLEGATE
Joe, you're getting to be a regular prima donna.

JOE

Why do they have to keep after me? Why can't I just play baseball, instead of sitting around answering a lot of questions? Making up things about my past.

APPLEGATE

It's all right. If you get in a jam you can always turn to me.

JOE

I don't want to get in a jam.

APPLEGATE

Also, it seems as though you sometimes forget who made you what you are today.

JOE

I'm batting 480.

APPLEGATE

As a baseball player you are a triumph. As a man who goes through with a bargain you leave something to be desired. I followed you last night.

JOE

(Surprised)

Oh.

APPLEGATE

And I followed you the night before.

JOE

Oh . . . Don't you just know where I am without all that effort?

APPLEGATE

No, Joe, I have to do most things the hard way. The only thing that's absolutely effortless is the cigarette trick. (*Grabbing lighted cigarette out of the air*) And now I'm trying to break myself of the filthy habit.

(*He coughs slightly.*)

JOE

Well is there any objection to my walking around where I used to live?

APPLEGATE

Yes. You know how I feel about home and wives.

JOE

That's why I didn't tell you I was going back. I love baseball, Mr. Applegate, but I'm homesick.

APPLEGATE

I'm planning some diversion for you. I have sent for a very attractive girl from Chicago.

JOE

(*Irritably*)

I don't like people from Chicago. I sold a house to a couple from Chicago once who . . .

APPLEGATE

Oh, nuts with that, Joe. I'm offering you a chance to know one of the most fascinating women ever known in the history of the world—

JOE

No, thank you!

APPLEGATE

Well, don't go back to Magnolia Street. Do you understand? I forbid it.

JOE

You don't own me yet—not until after midnight on the twenty-fourth.

APPLEGATE

And then?

JOE

Is it so terrible just to want to go home?

APPLEGATE

It's gauche. You're too big for that kind of sentimental nonsense. Now you just think things over.
(*He exits.*)

JOE

(*Calling after him*)
I am thinking things over. I'm thinking about a lot of things. (*Music. He sits and sings reflectively*)

A man doesn't know what he has until he loses it,
When a man has the love of a woman he abuses it.
I didn't know what I had when I had my old love,
I didn't know what I had 'til I said, "Goodbye, old love!"
Yes, a man doesn't know what he has 'til it is no longer
   around
But the happy thought is,
Whatever it is he's lost, may some day once again be found!

DAMN YANKEES

VAN BUREN
(Enters)
Joe—Mr. Welch wants to speak to you.

WELCH
(Enters behind VAN BUREN*)*
Joe.

JOE
Yes, Mr. Welch.

WELCH
Joe, Miss Thorpe hadn't quite finished talking to you. You don't mind, do you, lad?

JOE
I'll do whatever you say, Mr. Welch.

VAN BUREN
(Calling)
Come in.
(Reporters come in followed by GLORIA *and* APPLE-GATE.*)*

WELCH
(Sitting at his desk)
Joe's feeling better now if you've got any other questions—

GLORIA
(Aggressively)
It isn't that I've got more questions, Mr. Welch—but I don't think I caught the answer to the one I asked.

JOE

Which one?

GLORIA

Your family.

JOE

They've all passed away. I haven't any family. Nobody.

GLORIA

What about friends?

WELCH

Well, he's got one friend I know of. Put me down, little girl.

GLORIA

What about your friends back in Hannibal? Heard from any of them?
(APPLEGATE *steps out from the group of reporters.*)

APPLEGATE

If you will permit me to say a word. I happen to represent the Hannibal *Bugle* and I'm telling you right now that everybody in our little old town is just as proud as pumpkins of little old Joe.

GLORIA

Well, thank little old you. And thank little ol' Joe.

WELCH

(*Jumping up*)
Quit picking on the boy, will you? He hasn't got anything more to tell you. If you want to ask questions, ask me.

LYNCH

O.K. Do you think Washington is going to win the pennant?

(*The reporters laugh at this absurdity.*)

GLORIA

When I swim the channel.

REPORTER

Don't be so funny.

JOE

(*Losing his temper*)

What's so funny? What's so damn funny about Washington winning the pennant?

VAN BUREN

Now, Joe.

JOE

Who's winning more games than we are?

LYNCH

Well, Joe, I—

JOE

I don't know why it's such a funny idea that we should cop the pennant. All we have to do is win games.

WELCH

Hear. Hear.

JOE

(*Subsiding*)

I guess I talked too much.

WELCH

No, you didn't. These newspaper people don't know what it is to have your heart in a ball club. O.K., we're not even in the first division. But strange things happen in baseball. We're playing like a new team. We're climbing—we're moving up. So you think what you please and I'll think what I please. But don't blame me for hoping and don't blame me for loving this boy who's made it possible for me to hope. Now you can go out and put it in your papers that I say that we'll have the pennant sewed up by the twenty-fifth of September. (*Puts his hand on* JOE's *shoulder*) That's what we think isn't it, Joe?

JOE

The twenty-fifth. The season ends on the twenty-fifth?

WELCH

That's right, boy—

JOE

We'll have it sewed up by the twenty-fourth.

WELCH

Now there's a statement for you.
    (APPLEGATE *comes up behind* JOE *and whispers angrily.*)

APPLEGATE

How sneaky can a fellow get!

(*Blackout*)

Scene VI

LOLA *is discovered sitting on a bench in front of the* JOE
HARDY *billboard. She is filing her nails.* LOLA, *a beautiful red-
head, is just what the Devil ordered.*

APPLEGATE
(*Enters in a hurry*)

Lola.

LOLA

Hi ya, Chief.

APPLEGATE

Welcome to the nation's capital.

LOLA

Thank you, Chief.

APPLEGATE

Have a good trip?

LOLA

Perfect. The plane crashed in Cleveland.

APPLEGATE

Good, good. Now how about that job in Chicago?

LOLA

Cleared the whole thing up before I left. I got the old boy

to embezzle $100,000 and lost it for him at the race track. Then his wife left him and he took to drink. I told him I was through and he jumped out of the window. Twenty-second story.

APPLEGATE

That's high enough. That's fine.

LOLA

Want me to try the Empire State on the next one?

APPLEGATE

No, no, Lola. This is a straight seduction job. New boy I just got hold of. (*Restlessly pacing in front of her*) Look Lola, I've done a terribly foolish thing—I'm really ashamed to confess it. I let this real estate agent talk me into an escape clause.

LOLA

I never heard of it.

APPLEGATE

You'll never hear of it again. I've got too much on my mind. It slipped by me. I'm overworked.

LOLA

I know, poor dear, elections coming up.

APPLEGATE

So when I made this Joe Hardy deal, I . . .

LOLA

Joe Hardy?

APPLEGATE

That's his name.

LOLA

Gee, they say he's great. Clarence just raved about him.

APPLEGATE

Who's Clarence?

LOLA

You know—
(She puts her hands together and gestures diving motion.)

APPLEGATE

Look, Lola, here's the tie-up. This is a mass torture deal like the thirty-years war. I've got thousands of Washington fans drooling under the illusion that the Senators are going to win the pennant.

LOLA

(Enthusiastically)
Oh, Chief, that's awfully good. There'll be suicides, heart attacks and apoplexy. Just like the good old days.

APPLEGATE

But, the key to the whole thing is this fellow. He wants to go back to his wife. For all I know he's sneaking out there right this minute.

LOLA

Well, don't worry, Chief, you know I'm pretty good at

making men forget their wives. This is a routine case. I'll give him the standard vampire treatment.

(*Seductively rolls her shoulder.*)

APPLEGATE

There isn't a home-wrecker on my staff better than you, Lola. But this fellow's stubborn.

LOLA

Oh, c'mon, Chief. You know I've got what it takes. (*Music*) Don't make me brag.

(APPLEGATE *watches from sidelines as* LOLA *sings.*)

LOLA

(*Sings*)
I took the zing out of the king of Siam!
I took the starch out of the sails
Of the Prince of Wales,
It's no great art, gettin' the heart of a man
On a silver platter
A little brains—a little talent
With an emphasis on the latter!
I made mince-meat out of a sweet young farmer!
I knocked the fight out of a knight
When I pierced his armor
And I'll bet, I can upset every male
In a Yale regatta!
A little brains—a little talent
With an emphasis on the latta!
You gotta know just what to say and how to say it
You gotta know what game to play and how to play it

You gotta stack those decks with a couple-a extra aces
    (*Uses a handkerchief to emphasize her best features*)
And this queen has her aces
In all the right places!
I've done much more than that old bore, Delilah!
I took the curl out of the hair of a millionaire
There's no trick gettin' some hick who is cool
Just a little warmer.
A little talent—a little brains
With an emphasis on the former!
Split up a home, way up in Nome, Alaska!
And wrecked the life of every wife
Down in Madagascar
Ask me why weak men'll die for me
Strong men simply shatter
    (*Baby talks*)
A little brains—a little talent
With an emphasis on the latter!
You gotta know just what to do and how to do it
You gotta know what tea to brew and how to brew it
You've seen the sign that says George Washington once
    slept here,
Well tho' nobody spied him
Guess who was beside him?
Bring on that boy, he'll be a toy to Lola
Just one more case she can erase with that old boffola
What's my plan, same as with any man
I'll use the standard patter
Plus a little this-a—and a little that-a
With an emphasis on the—on the latter!
    (*Follows* APPLEGATE *off.*)

Scene VII

MEG's *house.* JOE *appears on porch.* MEG *comes in living room, goes to chair where there is a paper bundle.* JOE *watches through the screen door.*

SISTER

(Appears from the kitchen door)

Did you find them?

*(*JOE *ducks back against the wall.* MEG *takes a carton of eggs out of the bundle and passes it to* SISTER. DORIS *sticks her head in from the kitchen door.)*

DORIS

I need those eggs.

SISTER

Here.

(Passes them to her.)

DORIS

(Whispering to SISTER*)*

Get Meg to come with us.

(She closes door.)

SISTER

Yes, Megsie, after we finish the baking how about going on the town with us?

MEG

No, thanks.

SISTER

Megsie, you might as well face it, Joe is never coming back.

MEG

I like to pretend he is.

SISTER

Well, you got to go on living.

MEG

I am living.

SISTER

You know, living life to the full. Now you come with us. We're going down to the station to see Gregory Peck come in on the train from California.

(SISTER *exits to the kitchen.* MEG *straightens the papers.* JOE *knocks on door.*)

MEG

Come in. (JOE *enters, stands just inside door looking at her.* MEG *continues checking grocery list and then turns and sees that it is a stranger*) Oh. Oh, I'm sorry—I thought you were the deliveries.

JOE

No, I came about—that is—someone told me you had a room you might be willing to rent.

MEG

Me! Rent a room!

JOE

That's what they said—some fellow down at the corner. I'm looking for a nice quiet place.

MEG

My goodness. I never even thought of renting a room.

JOE

I wouldn't be any trouble—I can promise you that.

MEG

Well, I'm sure you wouldn't. But you see, mister—mister—

JOE

Joe Hardy.

MEG

My husband's name is Joe.

JOE

Is that so? That's quite a coincidence.

MEG

He's away.

JOE

Oh! That's too bad.

MEG

Yes.

JOE

For long?

MEG

Not too long—I hope. He had to go on a trip.

JOE

I guess that's why this fellow thought you might have an extra room.

MEG

I wonder who that could be.

SISTER

Meg!

MEG

Oh dear—excuse me. We're cooking for the bridge club— a friend of mine and her sister, from my home town. Just make yourself at home.

> (MEG *picks up bundle of groceries from chair, exits to kitchen.* JOE *looks over the room nostalgically, his chair, the television set, for a second. He is stunned seeing his reflection in the mirror. He sits.*)

JOE
(Sings)

But he'll come back to you again . . .

> (MEG *re-enters.*)

MEG

I'm sorry to have taken so long. (JOE *jumps up*) My friends think it will be good for me to take in a boarder. They are coming right in to meet you as soon as they fix their hair. I have a room that was my husband's den that we use as a guest room. It has a nice studio couch. Would you like to see it?

JOE
(Impulsively)

Oh, I know it's all right.

69

MEG

Better take a look at it. Oh, I'd have to ask you not to use the downstairs when I have bridge club. That's every three days.

JOE

Oh, that wouldn't bother me. I'd be away quite a bit, anyhow. I go away for like two or three weeks at a time.

MEG

Oh, I see.

JOE

You have to live in hotels when you're out on the road and you get kind of lonesome just to be in somebody's house. That's why I thought . . . You see I was just walking around the neighborhood wishing I could live out this way.

(*Music—creates the mood.*)

MEG

I guess I see through you. You just miss somebody that you've left behind. Is that it?

JOE

Yes, I do. I miss somebody something awful.

MEG

Well, I know how that is.

JOE

(*Singing*)

A man doesn't know what he has until he loses it,
When a man has the love of a woman he abuses it,

I didn't know what I had when I had my old love,
I didn't know what I had 'til I said, "Goodbye old love."
Yes, a man doesn't know what he has 'til it is no longer
    around
But the happy thought is
Whatever it is he's lost, may some day once again be found!

MEG

    (*Sits in chair and sings almost to herself*)
I know what you mean Joe,
Only too well
For I am lonely just like you.
Lonely for my Joe, my sweet Joe
How really sweet I never knew
I really never knew
    (*Rises and crosses to screen door*)
A woman doesn't know what she has until she loses it,
When a woman has the love of a man she abuses it,
I didn't know what I had when I had my old love,

JOE

I didn't know what I had 'til I said "Goodbye old love."
    (*Singing to her but she is looking off oblivious*)
Yes, a man doesn't know what he has 'til it is no longer
    around

BOTH

But the happy thought is,
Whatever it is he's/she's lost, may some day once again be
    found!
    (*After song they exit upstairs to look at the room.*

SISTER *and* DORIS *enter. They are transformed from their kitchen clothes—all dolled up for the mysterious stranger.*)

SISTER

(*Playing glamourously with a long silk scarf until she sees no one is there, then she drops her pose*)

Huh—not here.

DORIS

(*Seeing* MEG *coming downstairs*)

Oh, where is he?

MEG

(*Controlling her excitement*)

He's upstairs. He's going to take it. He's clearing out a couple of drawers.

SISTER

Don't you want us to look him over first? I thought you said . . .

MEG

I know I did—but you can just tell, he's such a nice boy. Look out, here he is. (*They all disburse and try to look casual.* JOE *re-enters down stairs*) I want you to meet my friends. This is Mr. Harper, Sister Miller—

SISTER

Hello there.

MEG

—And Doris Miller.

DORIS

How do you do.

72

SISTER

(*Making charming conversation*)
Isn't it a gorgeous day.

DORIS

(*Suddenly in a harsh whisper*)
Sister!

SISTER

What?

DORIS

Come here.

(*They draw to one side, whispering and looking at* JOE)

JOE

Look, Mrs. Boyd, here's a mighty funny thing. When I was clearing out that top drawer I found an envelope addressed to you.

MEG

You did? Well, that's strange. I thought I had looked everywhere after—Well now, what do you know about that. (MEG *opens envelope*) My gosh—look—money! Well say, you certainly have brought me luck. Look at this, kids. I guess Joe left that there and—

SISTER

(*Suddenly attacking* JOE)
You're Joe Hardy, aren't you?

JOE

(*Nods*)
I guess I am.

SISTER

(Out of control)

It's Joe Hardy, Meg. Not Mr. Harper. It's Joe Hardy. He's the greatest baseball player—oh, my goodness, I'm flabbergasted. Oh, gee, Joe Hardy. May I have your autograph?

(She takes autograph book from pocketbook and hands it to JOE.*)*

DORIS

You don't know what's happened to you, Meg, he's a hero!

SISTER

We saw the game and that home run you made in the seventh, was that an inside pitch? Was he trying to loosen you up? (APPLEGATE *enters porch*) Oh, yes, and that wonderful double play in the third. Did you hurt your hand?

(APPLEGATE knocks on screen door.)

MEG

(Opens door)

Yes—good morning.

APPLEGATE

(Flashes identification case—too quickly for her to read it)
I'm from City Hall.

MEG

(Baffled)

Where?

APPLEGATE

(Flashes case again)
City Hall. Just serving official notice in the neighborhood.

MEG

What kind of notice?

APPLEGATE

New zoning law. No one is permitted to take roomers in this neighborhood.
(JOE *talking to girls hears his voice, turns and comes slowly toward door.*)

MEG

But they do—people do.

APPLEGATE

Effective as of today.

JOE

What's this?

MEG

Why—this man.

JOE

It's all right, Meg. I mean Mrs. Boyd. I know this man—just let me talk to him. (*He comes out on the porch*) I'll be right in.
(MEG *enters and crosses with girls to desk upstage.*)

SISTER

What is it?

JOE

Really, Mr. Applegate, you're carrying things too far.

APPLEGATE

Joe, she's here. I have told her all about you. She's interested, know what I mean? A real sexy baby.

JOE

If you keep hounding me this way, I'm not going to be able to play worth a damn.

APPLEGATE

Do you think I like it? Wasting my time, not to mention the money spent on costumes.
(*He polishes brass badge on his hat.*)

JOE

Mr. Applegate, can't you understand how I feel?

APPLEGATE

No.

JOE

I was married when I was only twenty. No matter what went wrong with my life or my business there was always someone I could trust and a place to come to where I'd feel protected—this home—and I can't get over it all at once.

APPLEGATE

Joe, you're not trying.

JOE

And if you want to know I've rented a room here.

APPLEGATE

But I told you. (*Losing his temper he kicks chair and grabs his foot*) Oh, my hoof!
    (*Exits.*)

JOE
(*Enters living room*)

He's gone.

MEG
(*Turning to him*)

What did he say?

JOE

Oh, he's just a practical joker.

MEG

Oh. I'm not much of a judge of character. That's what my husband always said.

SISTER

(*Carrying a bunch of baseball pictures from desk*)
We're going to fix your room up with a lot of Joe's old baseball pictures—Mr. Hardy.

MEG

My husband's a great fan—you know.

SISTER

Oh, a fanatic. Every night in front of the television set you would see that big fat slob sitting there.

(*Blackout*)

Scene VIII

Corridor at the ball park. A bunch of players spill enthu-siastically across the stage from the field to the locker rooms.

BOULEY

Haven't had such a good time in years.

LOWE

Neither have I.

BRYAN

Lost it in the sun, he said.

SMOKEY

They're just another ball team, that's all.

MICKEY

We wuz in there today.

SMOKEY

Just like Benny told us.

ROCKY

Well, I hope them so called bombers enjoyed theirselves as much as I did tonight.

HENRY

Hey, you looked pretty near like a ball player today.

ROCKY

Three for five, kid, three for five.

(WELCH *enters with* VAN BUREN.)

WELCH

A lot of Joe's fan clubs want to do things that night. I asked Joe if he wanted this party. He said no, he only wanted to be in the Hall of Fame.

VAN BUREN

He was kidding.

WELCH

I don't think so.

VAN BUREN

A party for Joe is a good idea, but about a month from now. At the end of the season.

WELCH

Sometimes I think Joe is fourteen years old and sometimes I think he's fifty.

(*They exit.* APPLEGATE *enters, enjoying their last remark.* GLORIA *enters.*)

GLORIA

Well! I hear we finally got on television.

APPLEGATE

Does that surprise you?

GLORIA

I was wondering if you could tell me why he has been refusing to appear up to now.

79

APPLEGATE

Certainly, I would be glad to. He's like I am. He's shy.

GLORIA

Mr. Applegate, I'd like to ask you just one more question. When Joe was back in Hannibal, did he have the same name?

APPLEGATE

Yes, Hardy. You spell it with an H.
(*Laughs loudly.*)

GLORIA

What's so funny?

APPLEGATE

Something came to mind. It isn't important.

GLORIA

He played a nice game tonight.

APPLEGATE

His batting average went up four more points. Now it's 524, not bad for a raw rooky.

GLORIA
(*Exiting*)

Yes, very raw!

APPLEGATE

Lovely girl. I know she'll make some nice young man very unhappy.

(*Blackout*)

SCENE IX

*The locker room. A series of open lockers, each with a
name plate, are decorated with family pictures and newspaper clippings. Clothes hang in most of them and some even
have strings stretched across with socks hung up to dry.*

*In the darkness, before lights come up, we hear the ex-
uberant voices of the players.*

ROCKY

(Putting on shoe)
Three for five, kid, three for five.

SMOKEY

(Enters with towel draped around him)
Hey, Rocky, that dumb blonde tomato from the drugstore
is out there waiting for you.

ROCKY

Tell her to keep on chewing the gum and relax.

SMOKEY

She asked was I the reception committee.

SOHOVIK

(Calling after SMOKEY*)*
You're sure dressed for the part.

ROCKY

Did you see Dawson throw down his glove when I hit that three-and-two pitch?

HENRY

I swing at the ball, and the next thing I know I'm riding into third.

ROCKY

Senators nine, well-known Yankees two. You know what I'm going to do? I'm going to memorize that.

VAN BUREN
(*Enters*)

I was just talking to Mr. Welch, he's pretty pleased. (*Boys ad lib*) Get some sleep, boys. Tomorrow we'll pin their ears back in a bow knot for them.

(*Exits.*)

ROCKY

Three for five.

SMOKEY

(*Enters, this time wearing a wild sport shirt and wilder shorts which clash*)

Say, Rocky, the blonde is tired of gum. She wants something to eat.

SOHOVIK

I see you're receiving formal now.

(SMOKEY *exits.* JOE *enters from showers, wearing shorts and clogs with a towel thrown around his neck.*)

82

DEL

How'd she go, Joe?

JOE

Fine.

SOHOVIK
(*Tucking shirt in trousers*)
Yeah. What'd you tell the great invisible audience?

JOE

I told them we were lifting our mortgage on the second division and taking an option on first place.

ROCKY

You sound like one of them white collar workers.
(*For* JOE *an uncomfortable moment of silence.*)

JOE

Oh. I used to sell a little real estate. Just a side line.
(*Crosses to his locker and starts to dress slowly.*)

SOHOVIK

Every ball player should have a side line.

APPLEGATE
(*Enters*)
Good evening, gentlemen. Great game, Joe, proud of you, my boy.

BOYS

Good night, Joe. So long, Joe.

JOE

Night, fellows.

APPLEGATE

Well, Joe, we showed those Yankees, didn't we?
(*A few more players all duded up pass across.*)

JOE

If we could just take the double-header tomorrow,
wouldn't that be great?

APPLEGATE

You will, you will, I feel it in my bones. Joe, did you notice
that charming young lady sitting in the box with me?

JOE

Yeah, I saw her.

APPLEGATE

Wants to meet you. I'll bring her in.

JOE

Well, wait'll I get my pants on.
(*He starts to put on pants.*)

APPLEGATE

That's my boy.

JOE

Say, you know I got sort of a date . . . out home, I mean.
I know you don't like it.

APPLEGATE

Joe, I do like it. I've changed my mind. I want you to be happy.

JOE

Thanks.

APPLEGATE

But this girl is a sweet kid and she wants to meet you so . . .

JOE

Sure. Sure.

APPLEGATE

(*Calling off*)

Lola! (*To* JOE) She talked about you all through the game. Ah, here we are. (LOLA *slithers in around locker. She is all decked out for seduction. A sort of latter-day Sadie Thompson with a rose in her hair*) Joe, I want you to meet my friend, Lola.

JOE

How do you do?

APPLEGATE

This is Joe Hardy.

LOLA

(*She speaks with a thick Spanish accent.*)

I have seen him from a distance.

APPLEGATE

And admired him.

85

LOLA

You should not tell what I admire.

APPLEGATE

Joe, this is Señorita Lolita Rodriguez Hernando. You may have seen her picture in the papers. She was Miss West Indies of 1957.

JOE

Well, it's certainly a pleasure to meet you.

LOLA

Thank you.

APPLEGATE

Joe, keep Lola company for a second—I got to get a hot dog.

(*He turns and exits in a big hurry.*)

JOE

(*Looks after him as if to call him back, and then remembers Lola*)

Gee, where's my manners? Won't you sit down.

LOLA

You are so polite. (*She walks insinuatingly around the room*) This is where you all get ready?

JOE

Yes, ma'am.

LOLA

Interesting. The truth is, Mr. Joe, I do not know how to
talk to a man so famous like you.

JOE

How about you? Miss West Indies! That's going some.

LOLA

It is silly. I am ashamed he told you. Mr. Applegate tries to
show me off too much. (*Crosses and touches him*) Because
my picture is in the papers and because maybe I am pleasing
to look in a bathing suit, is that important?

JOE

Well, as the fellows around here would say, (*Laughs, self-
consciously*) it ain't bad.

LOLA

(*Protesting, she hangs onto his shirt*)
No, Joe. What is inside me, if I am an interesting person,
that is important.

JOE

Oh, I agree.

LOLA

(*Crossing to the side of the room, she points to suitcases on
top of lockers*)
Thank you. What is those?
(*She jumps up on bench to examine them.*)

JOE

That's where we pack our duffle when we go on the road.

LOLA

Oh, Joe—You like music? You like dancing?
(*She accompanies these questions with appropriate movements of the hips.*)

JOE

I'm not so very hot at dancing, but I like music. I studied cornet for three years.

LOLA

(*Looks down from bench as if from a precipice*)
You help me down, please?

JOE

Oh sure.
(*He offers hand, but she pulls him to her and puts arm around neck, then slides safely down him.*)

LOLA

(*Hanging on for dear life*)
Thank you.

JOE

(*Getting rattled*)
I really studied for four years. My teacher said I had a natural lip—uh—for cornet playing, that is. I mean to play the cornet you have to have good lips. Oh, gosh.
(*In panic he pushes himself away.*)

88

LOLA

Oh, Joe, you are wonderful boy.

JOE

I am?

LOLA

You are so honest.

JOE

I'm honest, but I'm dumb, too.

LOLA

I like people who do not brag about themselves.

JOE

Well, me too. I don't know where Mr. Applegate . . .

LOLA
(*Interrupting*)
Do you know you and I feel just alike about things.

JOE

We do?

LOLA

I think we shall become to know each other quite well. Joe, would you like to take me somewhere tonight?

JOE

Gee, I sure would like to, but you know what Mr. Van Buren would say.

LOLA

He'd say you lucky boy.

JOE

No, no, he'd say it's late. He likes us to get to bed early.

LOLA

Any particular place? (JOE *looks at her and she turns away coquettishly*) Oh, Joe, you think I am a naughty girl.

JOE

No. No, I don't. (*Crosses to locker and gets shoes*) Only you see I rented a room out in Chevy Chase this afternoon and I promised to move in tonight. I got to go home.

LOLA
(*Startled*)

Home.

JOE

Yes, I promised to be there.

LOLA

You want to hurt Lola's feelings?

JOE

No, no, I don't want to hurt anybody's feelings. That's why I . . .

LOLA

But Lola wants you to stay with her.

90

JOE
We have to keep training and strict rules and all that.

LOLA
You can tell me all their rules.

JOE
(Sits on box to tie shoelaces)
You're making this very complicated.

LOLA
Then be good boy.

JOE
I'm trying to.

LOLA
And do like Lola tells you to do. (*From upstage she points commanding finger at* JOE *and begins to sing*)

Whatever Lola wants
Lola gets
And little man, little Lola wants you.
Make up your mind to have no regrets,
Recline yourself, resign yourself, you're through.
I always get what I aim for
And your heart'n soul is what I came for.
Whatever Lola wants
Lola gets,
Take off your coat
Don't you know you can't win?
You're no exception to the rule,

I'm irresistible, you fool, give in! . . . Give in! . . . **Give in!**

> (*She lies seductively across a bench upstage and pantomimes talking over the telephone.*)
> (*She dances invitingly, removing first her gloves, and flowered hat, then peels off her skirt, and cavorts in a pair of tight-fitting lace toreador pants and from this she strips even further to tights. It is having its effect on* JOE.)

Hello, Joe
It's me.
He hits so far
—hold on—that's you.
   Aaah—Haaaaaa
   Poo poo pa doop
   Peek-a-boo
   Yoo-hoo
     (*Sings*)
I always get what I aim for
And your heart'n soul is what I came for
. . . Lola wants
. . . Lola gets
. . . You'll never win
I'm irresistible, you fool,
Give in . . . Give in . . . Give in.

> (*Finally she drapes herself across his lap.* JOE *uncomfortably rises and puts* LOLA *down on the box.*)

JOE

Lola.

LOLA

Yes, Joe.

JOE

If it was you I promised to come home to you'd want me to, wouldn't you?

LOLA

I see.

JOE

You're awfully wonderful and I wish I was two people, but I'm only one— and I'm married.

(*Makes a quick exit.*)

APPLEGATE

(*Enters behind lockers*)

What a flop. Just a routine case, eh?

LOLA

(*Dropping her Spanish accent*)

I was wrong. He is different.

APPLEGATE

Alibi Ike.

LOLA

I never ran up against one like that before.

APPLEGATE

Oh, bosh and double bosh. Get yourself a new line. Your methods are old-fashioned. Whatever Lola wants.

(*Takes out a handkerchief and jumps around in an imitation of her dance.*)

LOLA
(*Defiantly*)
All right, Chief. You just give me time, just give me . . .

APPLEGATE
There isn't any time. They go on the Western trip, but when he comes back, I'll smoke him out. When he gets back I'll start a scandal in the neighborhood. She'll have to throw him out.

LOLA
What kind of a scandal?

APPLEGATE
Good Lord, the boy is living right there in the house with that woman. Aren't you shocked? I am!

(*Blackout*)

Scene X

In front of black curtain. Girls and boys enter dressed to represent the various teams in the American League. Their costumes have a homemade but ingenious look.

TIMMY

You didn't need to get your costumes on yet. . . . what are you?

MARIE

Boston Red Sox.

BETTY

I'm a Detroit Tiger.

~~MISS WESTON~~

(Enters—busy organizer of the party)
Wait out there, please.
  (They start out.)

BETTY

   (Calling offstage)
Come on, Cleveland.

  (Three fans cross dressed in bright red long underwear and Indian headdresses.)

SISTER

(Enters with three kids carrying JOE HARDY *signs.* SISTER *is wearing a baseball hat. To* MISS WESTON)
Miss Weston, every fan club got to rehearse but us.

95

DAMN YANKEES

MISS WESTON _Doris_

All right, you may have the stage, but don't take too long.
(*Exits.*)

SISTER

Put down the sign, Jackie.

JACK _Colleen_

Don't I get to carry it?

SISTER

Not while we're singing.
(*He puts down a sign saying, "JOE, our hero."*)

RONNIE

What about our costumes?

SISTER

Later. Now line up. It's a big honor for us to be in the show
and we want to do well. (*Blows note on pitchpipe. They assume rigid formal pose as if rehearsing to an empty auditorium*) The Chevy Chase Fan Club is grateful to you, Joe,
because you taught us this big lesson.

ALL

(*Sing*)

You've gotta have heart,
All you really need is heart,
When the odds are sayin' you'll never win,
That's when the grin should start.

SISTER

(*Speaks*)
It's the youth of America, Joe.

96

DAMN YANKEES

CHERRY [handwritten: Margo]

(*Sings*)

When your luck is battin' zero.

SISTER [handwritten: Doris]

Get your chin up off the floor,

RONNIE [handwritten: Monty]

Mister you can be a hero

JACKIE [handwritten: Colleen]

You can open any door,

SISTER

There's nothin' to it, but to do it.

ALL

You've gotta have heart,
Miles 'n miles 'n miles of heart
Oh, it's fine to be a genius of course
But keep that old horse before the cart.

CHERRY [handwritten: Margo]

So when the bases are loaded

JACKIE AND RONNIE [handwritten: Monty + Colleen]

The count is three and two.

SISTER

You'll hit a homer, Joe, we can depend on you

ALL

You're a hero 'cause, you've got heart—
You've got heart—
You've got heart—
(*Exit.*)

97

Scene XI

As the curtain opens, the sound of hammering is heard. The lights come up on the stage of a hotel ballroom in preparation for a big night. The pillars and candelabra upstage are decorated with bunting and pictures of JOE HARDY. *There are a couple of ladders set up and a large banner leaning against a pillar.* WELCH *is discovered talking to* MISS WESTON *and* VAN BUREN.

WELCH

I'll make a little speech first—and then we'll bring on these acts, whatever they are. I hope you haven't got too many.

MISS WESTON Doris

No. There were about a hundred fan clubs that wanted to perform, but we just picked the best—

VAN BUREN

You'll give me a list?

MISS WESTON Doris

Oh yes—I have it in the dressing room.
(*An* ASSISTANT *enters.*)

ASSISTANT

Miss Weston—the G Street Fans can't find the costumes.

98

MISS WESTON

(*To* WELCH)

Excuse me, ~~Mr. Welch.~~

(*She hurries out with* ASSISTANT.)

WELCH

You feel all right about everything, do you, Benny?

VAN BUREN

I'm not bubbling over with joy about the games we played today, if that's what you mean.

WELCH

Well, don't show it. (VAN BUREN *gestures*) Let's make it a good party tonight. We've come to the end of the season better than I ever dreamed.

VAN BUREN

Two games to go.

WELCH

Now, now, you just relax, we'll be the champions. All we got to do is win one of those games.

VAN BUREN

But the way Joe cracked up on us today!

WELCH

(*Warning*)

Easy . . . easy. (JOE *enters carrying coat*) Well, boy, how's it feel to have the whole town honoring you?

JOE

Feels like I wish I deserved it.

VAN BUREN

Now, Joe boy, we'll show them tomorrow, hey?

MISS WESTON

(*Entering*)

Here's the list.
  (*Hands* VAN BUREN *list, and exits.*)

VAN BUREN

Oh, thanks.
  (*A couple of carpenters come on, pick up banner and begin to carry it off.*)

WELCH

Excuse us, Joe.
  (VAN BUREN *and* WELCH *exit.*)

JOE

I got to practice my speech.

  (*He sits on one rung of the ladder and mouths his speech. The banner upstage has by now been spread and reveals the slogan: Washington Saved His Country, Joe Saved Washington.* LOLA *enters from behind one of the pillars unseen by* JOE. *She climbs the other side of the ladder and perches, looking down amused at him. She is dressed in a costume version of a Washington baseball uniform with his number, 39, on the back of it.*)

LOLA

Congratulations.

JOE

(*Rising*)

Oh, it's you.

LOLA

(*Showing the number on her shirt back*)
I've become a fan—officially. We're putting a dance on in your honor tonight.

JOE

That's very nice, Miss Hernando.

LOLA

(*Jumps off ladder*)
No, Miss Hernando's gone. No accent. Didn't you notice? She failed dismally.

JOE

Kidding me again, I guess.

LOLA

No, Joe, just kidding myself. I'm just a bald hussy who just organized a fan club, without instructions from Mr. A.

JOE

He wanted us to lose today, didn't he? (*She shrugs*) Didn't you hear him giving me the razz all through the game—personal things—anything to put me off. That's why I threw the ball into the stands. I was trying to hit him.

LOLA

You let in two runs and hit an old lady. He was delighted.

JOE

What does he want?

LOLA

Tomorrow is the twenty-fourth.

JOE

Yes.

LOLA

I think he doesn't want to lose you.

JOE

And what do you want?

LOLA

I would like to be your friend.

JOE

I guess you mean it. Thanks.

LOLA

Joe, you make me feel girlish (*Sits*) and I'm 172 years old. You see, many men have loved me—hopelessly—but I felt nothing. And would you believe it, you're such a good, loyal, dumb, ordinary man, you make me feel tender? (*Carpenters enter*) It's quite exciting. You still believe me . . .

APPLEGATE'S VOICE

Oh, folderol.

LOLA

Look out!
(*She ducks behind a small sign on the chair. The carpenters have picked up the two other signs and have started to exit. The two small signs spell J and O.* LOLA *picks up E and follows them out.* APPLEGATE *and* GLORIA *enter.*)

APPLEGATE

Folderol, what business is it of yours where Joe lives?

GLORIA

I'm curious. That's all.

APPLEGATE

Joe moved out of that house in Chevy Chase because . . .
Why did you change to the hotel, Joe?

JOE

(*Defiant*)

To be near you. And let me tell you something else—we're going to win that pennant tomorrow. You wait and see.
(*Exits fast.*)

APPLEGATE

(*Calling after. Applauds*)

That's the spirit! (*To* GLORIA) That's the way a ball player should talk, don't you think?

GLORIA

I think a lot of things, my friend. You see I've just come back from a trip to Hannibal, Missouri.

APPLEGATE

Well, did you drop in and say hello to the boys at the *Bugle*?

GLORIA

There is no *Bugle*, Mr. Applejuice.

APPLEGATE

You know my name.

GLORIA

Yes, I do. But I don't know Joe Hardy's name.

APPLEGATE

What was that crack?

GLORIA

One thing I do know, his name isn't Joe Hardy.

APPLEGATE

If you are referring to the rumor that he is in reality Shifty McCoy, I deny it emphatically.
(*Sits on ladder rung.*)

GLORIA

(*Picking up the scent*)
Who's Shifty McCoy?

APPLEGATE

All right. If you haven't heard it, I haven't said it. (*Rises and talks to her across ladder*) What's your big problem anyhow? Why do you say he is not Joe Hardy?

GLORIA

Nobody in Hannibal has ever seen or heard of Joe Hardy. His birth is not registered there. He's a faker. Where'd he come from?

APPLEGATE

Oh, don't be so nosy. Go home. Get married. (*From behind pillar*) Have children.

> (*He disappears.* GLORIA *starts to write name in notebook, resting book on ladder.* MISS WESTON *comes in followed by carpenters.*)

MISS WESTON

Clear all these things, boys. (*Taking stepladder*) Excuse me.

GLORIA

> (*Calling offstage*)

Benny!

> (VAN BUREN *enters.*)

VAN BUREN

> (*Making notes on piece of paper*)

You part of this shindig?

GLORIA

Benny? (*Looking him over*) Hey, you're pretty. Benny, ever hear of a ball player named Shifty McCoy?

VAN BUREN

Isn't he the kid that took a bribe in the Mexican League about four years ago?

GLORIA

Oh?

VAN BUREN

Threw a game and they caught him at it.

GLORIA

What happened?

VAN BUREN

He took it on the lam. Never been heard of since as far as I know.

GLORIA

Did you know him?

VAN BUREN

No. No, Miss Thorpe, I remember seeing his picture in the paper at the time. It was quite a scandal.

GLORIA
(Snaps her fingers)
Of course, that's where I'll find it.
(MISS WESTON *enters.*)

MISS WESTON

Mr. Welch.

WELCH
(Appears, carrying notes)
I'm ready.
(Exits.)

GLORIA

(*Stopping* MISS WESTON)

Could you tell me where there's a phone? No, no, never mind.

(*She runs off.*)

MISS WESTON

We're going to start. Clear everybody.

(*Curtains close. A string of festive lights goes on, bordering the curtain. The orchestra plays a fanfare.* WELCH *comes on and talks directly to the audience.*)

WELCH

This is Joe's night, and I'm not going to start it off with any long speech. Later on you may have to listen to a tribute or two, but right now we're going to sit down and see what some of Joe's fan clubs think of him. Now this first number is by the "I Love Joe" fan club. Yes, that's what it says—and here they are.

(*Points across stage and exits.* LOLA *and one of the boys enter dressed in shiny black pants and colorful boleros. Both wear beat-up straw hats. They sing.*)

Ugh!
Who's got the pain when they do the mambo?
Who's got the pain when they go "Ugh"?
Who's got the pain when they do the mambo?
I dunno who—do you?
Who needs a pill when they do the mambo?
Who needs a pill when they go "Ugh"?
Who needs a pill when they do the mambo?

I dunno who—do you?
Someone must be sick with the heat?
Or steppin' on everyone's feet?
But if everyone's feeling O.K.
Why don't they just say "Olay"?
When the music carries them away! "Ugh!"?
Who's got the pain when they do the mambo?
Who's got the pain when they go "Ugh"?
Who's got the pain when they do the mambo?
I dunno who—do you?
Is there a doctor in the house?
Is there a doctor in the house?
If there's a doctor in the house,
Point him out,
For there is an element of doubt—as to
Who's got the pain when they do the mambo?
Who's got the pain when they go "Ugh"?
Who's got the pain when they do the mambo?
I dunno who—do you?

(*They finish the number in a frantic dance. After it is
over, fans dressed in their homemade costumes come
on stage applauding. LOLA and partner take a bow and
are congratulated by JOE. LOLA impulsively kisses him
on the cheek. The crowd oohs and aahs. LOLA is
shunted to one side of the stage and congratulated by
a group. During the next scene between APPLEGATE
and LOLA, a messenger appears with a note for VAN
BUREN and their conversation is in pantomime.*)

APPLEGATE

(*Sotto voce to* LOLA)
Going a little too far, don't you think?

LOLA

Didn't you like it?

APPLEGATE

I liked it fine! Puff him up! I'll bring him down again.

LOLA

You'll what?

APPLEGATE

(*Points to* VAN BUREN *and messenger*)
It's already started. Keep your eyes open, home-wrecker, you'll see who's got the pain.

VAN BUREN

Mr. Welch has just had a call from the Commissioner and that's one call we always answer. (*Crowd laughs*) And he asked me to take over. Now folks let's show Joe what we think of him.

(*The crowd lifts* JOE *on their shoulders and they start to sing.*)

Who came along in a puff of smoke?
Shoeless Joe from Hannibal Mo.
Strong as the heart of the mighty oak
(WELCH *enters, interrupts the song*)
Shoeless Joe from Hannibal Mo.

WELCH

(*Visibly shaken*)

Joe.

VAN BUREN

What's the matter?

WELCH

Joe, a very terrible thing has happened. In a few minutes
there will be an extra on the streets accusing you of being a
fellow who took a bribe down with the Mexican League.
(*Crowd ad libs*) QUIET! I want Joe to tell us it's not so.

JOE

Took a bribe?

WELCH

Yes, Joe.

JOE

I wouldn't do such a thing.

WELCH

The Commissioner has called a hearing for tomorrow
morning.

JOE

But who would say such a thing about me?

WELCH

If you can clear yourself, you can play, otherwise not.

JOE

(*Trying to quiet the crowd, he builds in determination*)
They gotta let me play. They gotta! Listen, everybody.
You've got to believe me. I'm not any crook. I'd die for the
team. And I will, and we'll win. We've got to win.
(*The theme of "A Man Doesn't Know" swells up from
the orchestra, drowning out his last words.*)

Curtain

ACT TWO

ACT TWO

Scene I

The curtain rises on the locker room. It is pre-game time and the entire team is massed. VAN BUREN *is holding forth.*

VAN BUREN

The whole town is behind Joe—parades—speeches. They know an O.K. guy when they see one. And so do I.

SMOKEY

Joe ain't done nothin' wrong.

HENRY

Mexican League—phooey!

VERNON

That wise Thorpe dame. She oughtta be run outta town.

SOHOVIK

Yer damn right.

VAN BUREN

Joe's up there with the Commissioner right now trying to clear himself.

SMOKEY

I bet the Yankees are behind this whole thing.

113

HENRY

Yeah, you tell 'em.

ROCKY

Yeah. They're scared of us.

VAN BUREN

Now listen. Whether Joe's with us today or not, you boys are going out there and play red-hot baseball.

ALL

Sure—right—etc.

VAN BUREN

We're the best club in the league and you know it. Now when we take the field, I want you to forget about Joe and go out there and fill the park with so many base hits those Cleveland Indians will think it's the Third World War!

(VAN BUREN *exits.*)

SOHOVIK

Benny's right.

HENRY

We got to forget about Joe and just think about the game.

ROCKY

You can't play good if you're worryin'—I found that out.

SMOKEY

That's why I got this outside hobby—somebody give me a four-letter word for—you can do it to an egg.

SOHOVIK

What did the Cleveland Indians do to us yesterday?

SMOKEY

They murdered us.

VERNON

Nix on that stuff.

SOHOVIK

Beat!

MICKEY

Talk about something cheerful, will you.

HENRY

Yeah. Women.

ROCKY

No women. You forgettin' the rules?

HENRY

No. But I ain't forgettin' women either.

ROCKY

Benny says if we're going to suceed in the big league we got to pay attention to all them strict rules.

MICKEY

Well, he's right.
(*All assent.*)

ROCKY

No drinking, no women—no late hours, no women. (*Music*) You got to keep your mind on the game.
(*Sings*)

We've got to think about the game!

ALL

The game, the game!
We've got to think about the game,
The game, the game!
Booze and broads may be great,
Though they're great they'll have to wait,
While we think about the game!

ROCKY

There was that waitress back in Kansas City,
Built for comfort, dumb but pretty!

ALL

Yeah? Yeah?

ROCKY

Man, her perfume sure did smell sweet,
Got her up to my hotel suite!

ALL

Yeah? Yeah?

ROCKY

She killed a pint of gin more or less,
The lights were low and she slips off her dress!

ALL

Yeah? Yeah? Yeah? Yeah?

ROCKY

But then I thought about the game!

ALL

The game, the game!

ROCKY

Oh, yes I thought about the game!

ALL

The game, the game!

ROCKY

Though I got the lady high,
I just left her high and dry,
Cause I thought about the game!

ALL

He thought about the game!

SMOKEY

There was the pullman car that I got lost in,
On a sleeper out of Boston!

ALL

Yeah? Yeah?

SMOKEY

Compartment doors all look the same there
Walked in one and there's this dame there!

ALL

Yeah? Yeah?

SMOKEY

Blonde, and stacked, and absolutely bare,
And nothin' separatin' us but air!

ALL

Yeah? Yeah? Yeah? Yeah?

SMOKEY

But then I thought about the game!

ALL

The game, the game!

SMOKEY

Oh, yes I thought about the game,

ALL

The game, the game!

SMOKEY

Though my heart said stay for tea,
All I said was pardon me!
Cause I thought about the game!

ALL

He thought about the game!

MICKEY

When a chick gives you the eye, remember—

ALL

Abstain!

DAMN YANKEES

LOWE

When you're dyin' for some rye, remember—

ALL

Refrain!

HENRY

If you're losin' at crap and the clock says it's eleven,
And suddenly each roll you roll—"huh"—comes up a seven,
And you're in the kind of dive, where men are men,

ALL

Be polite, say good night, you should be in bed by ten!

SMOKEY

When your mother bakes you cakes, remember—

ALL

Stay thin!

ROCKY

When you're kissin' till it aches, remember—

ALL

Don't give in!
Every rule we shall obey to be sure,
Cause to win we've gotta stay, good and pure,
Good and pure! Mumm.

SMOKEY

Hey, Rock, remember those twins we took a ride with,
Operatin' side by side with,

ALL

Yeah? Yeah?

SMOKEY

We're out of gas three miles from Philly,

ROCKY

The night is warm, the sky's a dilly,

ALL

Yeah? Yeah?

ROCKY

So I suggest we sleep beneath a tree,

SMOKEY

No one's there but Rock, the chicks and me.

ALL

Yeah? Yeah? Yeah? Yeah?

SMOKEY

So there we are, lyin' side by side under the tree.

ROCKY

Four minds with a single thought.

SMOKEY

I look at my girl,

ROCKY

I look at mine.

SMOKEY

Then with one fell swoop—
(*Boys clasp hands over* SMOKEY's *and* ROCKY's *mouths.*)

ALL

But then they thought about the game!
The game, the game!

ROCKY AND SMOKEY

Oh, yes we thought about the game!

ALL

The game, the game!
To our women one and all,
We will see you in the fall,
But for now we've got to stall,
Every dame!
And think about the game!
Think about the game,
Think about the, think about the, think about the, think
    about the,
Think about the game!

(*Blackout*)

Scene II

Curtain representing a park at dusk. There is a bench to one side of stage. Three girls enter and cross.

JANET

Sure the Senators lost today, they didn't have Joe.

JANIS

Tomorrow's the one that counts.

JOAN

The tickets were all sold out long ago.
> (JOE *enters while they are talking. He is wearing dark glasses and looks nervously in both directions.* MEG *enters.*)

MEG

Oh, Joe.

JOE

Meg.

MEG

Thanks for coming.

JOE

They postponed the hearing till ten o'clock tonight.

122

MEG

I didn't know whether it was all right for me to phone you.

JOE

Of course, it was all right.

MEG

Joe, I had something to explain. (*They sit*) If I'd known you were going to be in all this trouble, I wouldn't have asked you to give up your room. I want you to know that. I wouldn't care how much people talked.

JOE

I guess it was for the best. This is the twenty-fourth. It'll all be over soon.

MEG

You mean the baseball season?

JOE

Everything.

MEG

How you talk. Everything what?

JOE

We play the Yankees tomorrow for the pennant. If I shouldn't be in the game, would you think I was a crook?

MEG

Well, of course I wouldn't.

123

JOE

Do you think I'm Shifty McCoy?

MEG

I know you're not. It's silly. You're not the least bit Shifty, you're moody. Now if they called you Moody McCoy, then I'd think there might be some grounds.

JOE

At least I want to have my name cleared before I disappear.

MEG

What in goodness' name are you talking about?

JOE

There's a witness coming from Mexico City who knew Shifty McCoy. He's coming to the hearing tonight and then I'll be proved innocent.

MEG

Of course, you are. You're a good boy, I know that.

JOE

Do you? Do you think I came from Hannibal, Missouri?

MEG

No, Joe, I don't, but it's just as Sister said, if you want to pretend you did then you must have your reasons, and it's an honor to the town. But I know you're good. I may not be a judge of character, but I know when somebody's good. That's why I keep saying that Joe, the other Joe, will come back. (*Music sets the tone*) Because he was a good man too. And now that you're gone, I miss him more than ever.

JOE

He will come back.

MEG

You don't have to cheer me up.

JOE

He's closer than you think.

MEG

What would you know about it?

JOE

That's all right. Just remember what I said.
(*He sings*)

He's near to you
Near to you
Though you think he's far away
He's near to you, so near to you
As near as April is to May!
Can't you feel him there in his favorite chair
Staring at the fireplace
Oh so near to you, always near to you
Why you might as well be face to face
(*Rises*)
For it's just as though he were standing as close as I
I know it's hard to imagine, but try,

(MEG *steps away in thought*)
If he's really near to you, near to you
You may be far apart and yet
If he's in your heart
Really in your heart
How near to you can he get?

MEG

He's near to me, near to me
Even though he's far away
He's near to me, oh so near to me
As near as April is to May
(*Speaks*)
Joe used to take me dancing at the Elks. He wasn't such a hot dancer. We had lots of fun.

JOE

I'm not such a hot dancer either—
(*He bows to her.*)

MEG

I'd love it.
(*He leads her in a couple of waltz turns and stops.*)

JOE
(*Sings*)
If he's really dear to you,

MEG

He's near to me

JOE

You may be far apart and yet

126

DAMN YANKEES

If he's in my heart

Really in your heart
How near to you

How near to me

How near to you/me can he get?

(Blackout)

Scene III

APPLEGATE's *apartment. A flamboyant conglomeration of satin drapes, silk spreads and a canopied bed decorated with a large cherubic figure. There is a television set in the rear. There are elaborate French windows to one side of the stage and an entrance on the other.* LOLA *is sitting on* APPLEGATE's *bed watching him pace jubilantly.*

APPLEGATE

It's just psychology, baby, just psychology. Do you think this noble young Joe Hardy will desert his team and the men who have trusted in him? Never!

LOLA

But suppose.

APPLEGATE

You're not supposed to suppose: I've put a lot of effort into this case

LOLA

Well, he's an interesting boy.

APPLEGATE

And once I've got him for keeps, I'll make him throw the game. That'll kill him.

128

LOLA

As for me, I'm sorry.

APPLEGATE

(*Sharply*)

What did you say?

LOLA

I said I'm sorry for him.

APPLEGATE

I have observed of late a certain laxity on your part. Are you forgetting every principle I've ever taught you? All right —one hundred times.

LOLA

(*Cowed, begins to recite*)

Never feel sorry for anybody—never feel sorry for anybody.

APPLEGATE

I must select something appropriate for this evening's hearing. That looks terrible. I'll wear that.

LOLA

Never feel sorry for anybody. Never feel . . .

(*Knock on door.*)

APPLEGATE

Now can anybody guess who that is? (*Calling*) Come in, Joe.

(JOE *enters.*)

LOLA

(*Reciting automatically*)
Never feel sorry for anybody—never feel sorry for anybody.

APPLEGATE

All right, Lola, knock it off. Later. We've got the greatest baseball player in the world here—let's do him homage.

JOE

It's very kind of you to say that, Mr. Applegate. But it doesn't look as though Joe Hardy would ever make the Hall of Fame.

APPLEGATE

One can never tell.

JOE

I've made my decision, Mr. Applegate. That's what I came to tell you about. I would like to exercise the escape clause which was to take place on the twenty-fourth which is today.

APPLEGATE

Aren't you being a little hasty?

JOE

I thought it all over. I found that there is something more important in life than being a hero.

APPLEGATE

Deep this boy. Very deep.

JOE

I want out—I want to go back.

APPLEGATE

Very well. An operation of this kind has to take place at the witching hour. So, at five minutes to midnight if you still want to go back, say the word.

JOE

Suppose the hearing is still going on—you going to change me right there in front of everybody?

APPLEGATE

Oh, no. That would cause talk. No! All you have to do is say, "let's step into the next room." Joe Hardy will go through that door. He will never return—took it on the lam, they'll say.

JOE

I just wanted to be sure there was no misunderstanding. (*Crosses to door and turns*) Good-bye, Lola.
(*He exits.*)

LOLA

(*Drained of emotion*)
Never feel sorry for anybody—never feel sorry for anybody.
. . .

APPLEGATE

All right, Lola. Let's not just have the letter, let's have the spirit.

LOLA

(*Defiantly*)
Never feel sorry for anybody. Never feel sorry for anybody.

DAMN YANKEES

(Picks up tie on bed, and starts to put it on)
And don't get too impudent with me or I'll degrade you
and get Clementine in here for this work. *(Puts on coat)* Get
too fresh with me and I'll put you back on your broom. Now,
while I go to the hearing, you sit down over there and you
think of three dirty tricks. And they'd better be good. What's
the matter with you—huh? You discourage me. *(Music. He
walks toward the audience as curtains close behind him.
Sings)*

Whenever I'm from time to time depressed
And a trauma wells and swells
Within my breast
I find some pride deep inside of me
As I fondly walk the lane of memory
I see Bonaparte
A mean one if ever I've seen one
And Nero fiddlin' thru that lovely blaze
Antoinette, dainty queen, with her quaint guillotine
Ha ha ha ha
Those were the good old days
I see Indians draggin'
An empty covered wagon
When scalping the settlers was the latest craze
And that glorious morn, Jack the Ripper was born
Ha ha ha ha
Those were the good old days.
    (Hands in pockets)
I'd sit in my rockin' chair so peacefully rockin' there
Counting my blessings by the score
The rack was in fashion, the plagues were my passion

Each day held a new joy in store.
   (*Speaks*)
Was anybody happy?
   (*Sings*)
I see cannibals munchin' a missionary luncheon
The years may have flown but the memory stays
Like the hopes that were dashed when the stock market
   crashed
Ha ha ha ha
   (*Open arms*)
Those were the good old days
   (*Kneels and sings Mammy style*)
I'd walk a million miles or more
For some of the gore
Of those good
Old
Days!
   (*Exits.*)

Scene IV

COMMISSIONER'S *office. A hearing is in session.* WELCH, JOE, VAN BUREN, POSTMASTER *and various witnesses and reporters jam the room.* GLORIA *has the floor.* APPLEGATE, *in the extremely formal garb of a barrister, sits listening.*

GLORIA

Well, I'll tell you, because I value the good name of baseball more than I do a victory for my own team.

WELCH

Well, just because a picture in the paper taken four years ago happens to look something like him—

COMMISSIONER

Mr. Welch—

WELCH

I know, I know.

COMMISSIONER

Miss Thorpe has the floor.

POSTMASTER

Well, he never lived in Hannibal—that much I'll promise you.

COMMISSIONER

Not just now.

POSTMASTER

That paper paid my expenses to come down here and testify.

COMMISSIONER
(*Severely*)
Not just now. Sit down, please. Mr. Hardy.

JOE

Yes sir.

COMMISSIONER

Tell me— boy—if you were brought up in Hannibal, how do you account for the fact that nobody seems to remember you? Just give your explanation of that fact.

APPLEGATE
(*Rises*)
If I may interject a word. . . . Out in Hannibal, Missouri, comes this young woman, subtle, sophisticated, she approaches this simple man here—

POSTMASTER
(*Rises*)
Who's simple? Wait a minute now—

GLORIA

Mr. Commissioner. I would like to have one question answered by this Mr. Applegate. If, as you say, Joe Hardy was born in Hannibal, Missouri—why is there no record of his birth?

APPLEGATE

You have asked a question.

GLORIA

I have.

APPLEGATE

And I will answer it.

GLORIA

Thanks ever so.

APPLEGATE

And it will bring the blush of shame to your fair brow and a tear to many an eye—Joe's birth was not registered because his parents were not married. (*Bows head*) I hope you're satisfied.

> (*There is a second's pause and then* JOE *grabs himself in a motion of extreme embarrassment.*)

COMMISSIONER

Yes, yes, we will drop that line of inquiry.
> (*Secretary enters with note. Takes it to* APPLEGATE.)

APPLEGATE

I hope this remorseless inquisition has now reached its climax and—(*Reads note*) Oh. Good news. My witness from Mexico City will be here in thirty minutes.

JOE

(*Looks at watch*)

Thirty minutes! I can't wait. It's a quarter of twelve now.

GLORIA

Mr. Commissioner, I've got to say one thing—I've got to make one thing clear—I've been jeered and abused because I wrote that story—but I didn't originate the rumor about Shifty McCoy—I heard it from someone else.

VAN BUREN

Well, who?

GLORIA

That platitudinous manager of our young phenom—from Mr. Applegate

(*There is general confusion from the spectators, out of which we hear:* WELCH: *Applegate, that's impossible.* JOE: *He told you that?* POSTMASTER: *What are they talking about?*)

COMMISSIONER

Quiet please. Mr. Applegate? Do I understand?

APPLEGATE

That is one of the most dastardly misrepresentations.

COMMISSIONER

Just answer the question.

APPLEGATE

I am called here to answer questions; instead, let me ask a

question. When my time is needed to fight graft and corruption in organized baseball—why am I called upon to quibble with these fellow travelers?

(*There is a noise.* MEG, SISTER *and* DORIS *push through crowd.*)

MEG

We came here to witness.

COMMISSIONER

If you please—

GUARD

Just a second, lady.

DORIS

We're with Mrs. Boyd.

SISTER

(*Tearing loose from guard*)
Take your hands off me, you Republican.

COMMISSIONER

If you please.

MEG

We've decided that we should speak up.
(*She crosses to desk.*)

SISTER

We're material witnesses.

MEG

Why, hello there, Mr. Hawkins.

POSTMASTER

How are you, Meg?

MEG

It's the Miller girls.

POSTMASTER

Hello there, girls, how are you all?

COMMISSIONER

You seem to be old acquaintances.

MEG

We'd like to take the stand and testify.

SISTER

We'll take the oath or anything.

MEG

You see, at first we didn't remember Joe, and then when I
remembered him and I reminded the girls, then pretty soon
they remembered him too.

SISTER

Hello there, Joe. My, I just hardly know you now you've
grown up so.

WELCH

You knew him?

SISTER

We picked huckleberries together.

MEG

You must remember him, Mr. Hawkins. Don't you mind he used to come in and collect the mail for old Mrs. Peeper?

JOE

It's five minutes before midnight.

COMMISSIONER

What is it, Mr. Hardy?

JOE

I'd like to go in the other room and speak to Mr. Applegate.
(JOE *starts to exit.* MEG *puts her hand out and stops him.*)

MEG

Wait Joe, he remembers.

POSTMASTER

Sure, now I remember him.

WELCH

I knew it. I knew that Joe wouldn't lie.
(*The whole hearing room bursts into an uproar.*)

COMMISSIONER

Silence—silence! Quiet, please!

WELCH

That boy sat right there and let them call him a liar to his face and now, by God, he's vindicated.
(*Reporters start out.*)

COMMISSIONER

I don't want anyone to leave the room.

WELCH

I said to Benny Van Buren this morning, I said, "I know the boy—he's true blue." I know a loyal player when I see one. Why, I says, "That boy would go to hell for his team."
(*The clock starts to strike twelve.* JOE *turns quickly to* APPLEGATE. MEG *stops him.*)

SISTER

You bet he would, Mr. Welch. That's exactly what Meg said, didn't you?

MEG

Yes sir, Mr. Welch—'cause we didn't care what the papers said, we never lost faith in Joe. He may have come from—a poor family, but that's no sign of disgrace in this day and age. Certainly some of the greatest men in our country came from poor families. And the way it's turned out, some of the greatest baseball players did too. You see, we three all knew each other when we were young back in Hannibal and Mr. Hawkins knew us, so when we heard about this thing, we couldn't bear to see an injustice done and that's why we pushed through—although the corridors are so crowded I just thought we'd never make it—but we did.

(*During* MEG's *speech the curtain has slowly closed and the lights dimmed.*)

Scene V

In the black, a spotlight picks out a bench. JOE *enters slowly, sits dejectedly.* LOLA *enters a second later and stands beside him.*

LOLA
(Softly)

Joe.

JOE
(Looks up)

Oh! Where is he?

LOLA

He's asleep. I gave him a pill.

JOE

Why didn't you give him two?

LOLA

I did. Move over.

JOE
(Moving over)

Why not? We're both in the same club now.
(He leans over—his hands over his eyes. She sits very still, watching him.)

143

LOLA

Don't cry, Joe.

JOE

You should have been there. Mr. Welch said, "I know this boy—he'd go to hell for the team." Don't you think that's funny?

LOLA

You're going to win, Joe.

JOE

Maybe.

LOLA

I fixed it for you. I said I gave him two pills. I gave him four. He was so delighted with himself and horsing around and he said, "Give me a drink of demon rum." You know—big joke. So I did and I slipped four pills into it. He won't wake up until after the game.

JOE
(Rising)

But I wanted him to be there. I wanted him to have to sit right there and watch us win the pennant.

LOLA
(Rising)

If he were there you wouldn't win.

JOE

Benny's putting me in center field. I wouldn't hear him yell at me out there. I wouldn't even look at him.

LOLA

It wouldn't make any difference—he owns you now.

JOE

(*Sits*)

Oh. I see. I didn't know how it worked—Lola—what were you?

LOLA

(*Sits*)

I was the ugliest woman in Providence, Rhode Island.

JOE

He'll be good and sore at what you did. Will he turn you back?

LOLA

He threatens.

JOE

Two lost souls. I don't know whether to cry or make jokes.

LOLA

Oh, Joe—jokes. Make jokes. We're together tonight and maybe never again.

JOE

Then we ought to make the best of it.

145

LOLA

Please.

JOE

How do we do that?

LOLA

(*Putting her head on* JOE's *shoulder*)
You think of some way.
(*Music begins.*)

JOE

(*Putting his arms around her*)
Just give me a second now. I'll figure something out. I got it. (*They kiss*) Now what's the next step?

LOLA

(*Assuming her Spanish accent*)
Joe, would you like to take Lola some place tonight?

JOE

(*Coming out of his mood. He rises, lifts* LOLA *to her feet*)
Yes I would. It took me a long time, didn't it?
(*They start to walk off arm in arm.*)

LOLA

(*Happily*)
You like music? You like dancing?

JOE

Yes!
(*Both are laughing, on exit.*)

146

Scene VI

Night club. A semicircle of banquettes, a bandstand with a three-piece combo, a rather garish canopy overhead through which we see the stars. The effect is smoky and through the haze we see couples dancing. LOLA *and* JOE *are discovered at one table, surrounded by his fans.*

LOLA

Please, no more questions about the game. Tonight, we're here to have fun.

GIRL

So are we.

LOLA

That's what I mean—everybody have fun.

ANOTHER GIRL

They're only relaxing.

JOE

We sure are!
(LOLA *and* JOE *embrace, kiss.*)

GIRL

They're only human.

JOE AND LOLA
(*Sing*)
Two lost souls on the highway of life

(*Hold hands, look at each other*)
We ain't even got a sister or brother,
But ain't it just great, ain't it just grand?
    (*Pick up glasses, toast each other and drink*)
We've got each other!
Two lost ships on a stormy sea
One with no sails and one with no rudder
But ain't it just great, ain't it just grand
    (*They down another*)
We've got each udder!
Two lost sheep, in the wilds of the hills
    (LOLA *rises, drapes arms over* JOE)
Far from the other Jacks and Jills, we wandered away and
    went astray
But we ain't fussin'
Cuz we've got "us'n"
We're two lost souls on the highway of life
    (*He pulls her into his arms*)
And there is no one with whom we would ruther
Say, "Ain't it just great, ain't it just grand?"
    (*They drink again*)
We've got each other!
Wherever we go, whatever we do
As long as you've got me, and I've got you
We've got a lot
Because we've got each other.
    (JOE *and* LOLA *dance exultantly, arms around each
    other.*)

SPECTATOR

Hey, Joe, you call that dancing?

DAMN YANKEES

(General laughing. JOE *and* LOLA *separate, dragging the dancers, one by one, into the dance with them.)*

JOE AND LOLA

We ain't fussin'—cause we got "us'n."

(By the end of the dance, JOE *is playing the cornet, and* LOLA *and the fans have worked themselves up to a pitch of excitement as the curtain closes.)*

Curtain

Newscast again

Scene VII

The JOE HARDY billboard. Two fans cross.

FIRST FAN

We'll never see the game if we don't line up tonight.

SECOND FAN

Fella told me there were two or three hundred guys out there already.

> (DORIS *and* SISTER *enter. They are dressed in raincoats and galoshes and are carrying blankets and banners and paper bags with food to last them the wait on line.*)

DORIS

I think it's crazy.

SISTER

We'll be perfectly comfortable, we're ready for anything.

DORIS

Sleeping with a lot of men.

SISTER

That's a crude way to put it, Doris—sleeping in line with a lot of men would be more refined. Oh. Gosh!

> (*Her blanket unrolls, she stoops to fix it.*)

150

DORIS

Suppose some strange man tries to talk to us.

SISTER

That would be nice. But wouldn't it be better with two strange men—one for you, too.

DORIS

A pick-up!

SISTER

Doris, you make me sick, you're always saying we should live, and now we have a chance for a little social contact and you want to back out.

DORIS

I want to live, but in the daytime.

SISTER

Some of the best living is done at night, believe me.
(*Two men enter, pass the sisters.*)

BRYAN

They were just trying to keep Joe out of the game. The whole thing was a frame-up.

LOWE

Those dames from Hannibal sure told them. Those three old ladies ought to get a medal.
(*They exit.*)

SISTER

Old ladies. Oh well, it doesn't matter.

DORIS

It's what we get for lying.

SISTER

A little white lie for an important thing like the pennant is
nothing to be ashamed of.

DORIS

No, I suppose not.

SISTER

Because if we lose, I'm going to kill myself!
(*They exit.*)

(*Blackout. In the darkness* MEL ALLEN's *voice is heard coming
over the radio.*)

RADIO SPEECH: *Rhubarb*

Well, the rhubarb's over and Van Buren comes back to the
dugout. It's the first half of the eighth inning. Washington
leads four to three. The New York Yankees have a potential
tying run on second base, and boy how they'd like to bring
that runner home. All right, we're all set to go once again.
There's the stretch, check to the runner leading off second
base. Here comes the pitch. There's a long drive going deep
into left field, and it is fouled by three feet.

SCENE VIII

Billboard. A group of children discovered gathered around a portable radio.

BOY

Foul—it's a foul!

(APPLEGATE *and* LOLA *enter.* APPLEGATE *putting on tie,* LOLA *carrying his coat.*)

APPLEGATE

You knew I had to get to the game.

LOLA

(*Helping him on with his jacket*)
I tried to wake you. I shook you and shook you.

APPLEGATE

You lie. I see it all now. You doped me. But why? Why did you do it?

LOLA

Because I love him!

(APPLEGATE *takes a swipe at her and misses.*)

APPLEGATE

Love!

(*Cheer from the group of children.*)

APPLEGATE

(*To the children*)
What happened?

GIRL

Martin tried to steal second.

BOY AND GIRL

They got him! They got him!

BOY

Good old Smokey. He's got the arm for you!

APPLEGATE

What's the score?

BOY

Four to three Washington!

APPLEGATE
(*To* LOLA)
Well, I'll get there in time—Washington will lose—even if
I have to change him back right in front of everybody.

LOLA

Well, I don't want to see it.
(LOLA *runs out.*)

APPLEGATE

Come here. Come back here you.
(*He raises his hands in a magical gesture and we
hear the Devil's eerie music. Blackout. In the darkness*
MEL ALLEN's *voice is heard.*)

DAMN YANKEES

Coming up now for the Yankees is Hank Bauer. On deck Mickey Mantle. It's the first half of the ninth inning, one away, nobody on. The Senators now just two outs away from the pennant. Hank Bauer steps into hitting position. Hollingsworth out on the mound looks in to get his sign.

All set to go. He swings into the wind-up, around comes the right arm, in comes the pitch. Bauer swings, there's a hard hit ground ball going into the hole between third and short. Sohovik charges over, back hands the ball beautifully, there's the long throw—

Scene IX

Dugout and stands. Suddenly two banks of night lights are focused on the audience. We see the stands jammed with shouting people. VAN BUREN *is watching the game. He gives instructions to* SMOKEY *who runs off. The entire effect is that the audience is at the ball game.* APPLEGATE *and* LOLA *enter the stands.* LOLA *has been transformed into an ugly old harridan. They take their seats.*

APPLEGATE
(To fan)
What's the score? What's the score, bud?

FIRST FAN
Four to three, Washington.

SECOND FAN
(Ecstatically)
Come on Nats. We got 'em now!
(LOLA *belts at* APPLEGATE *with a scarf.*)

THIRD FAN
Mickey Mantle at bat. Get this guy—get this bum.

APPLEGATE
(Rises)
Come on, Yankees.

156

VAN BUREN

Back Joe, play deep.

LOLA

(*In a witchlike voice*)
Come on, Washington. Come on, Joe.
(*The crowd jumps to its feet.*)

VAN BUREN

Come on, Joe. (APPLEGATE *makes magical pass—more eerie music*) What's happened—what's the matter—come on, boy.

FIRST FAN

He can't run. He's lame or something.

VAN BUREN

Come on, boy, come—
(*The crowd is poised in suspense. Finally:*)

VAN BUREN

(*Shouts*)
He caught it!
(*The crowd goes wild, descends from the grandstand in masses and there is much leaping about and cheering.* LOLA *is left alone in the stands waving a scarf.*)

Scene X

Corridor at the ballpark. Tremendous noise from stands.
JOE HARDY *appears, only this time transformed back into the*
middle-aged JOE BOYD, *and is bursting out of his baseball*
suit. He runs frantically, trips and falls, gets up and runs off.
He is followed by a cheering swarm of Washington players
and fans.

VERNON

We won, we won!

SMOKEY

American League champions, that's what we are, American League champions.

ROCKY

We showed those New York dudes. (*Hugs* SMOKEY) You
was great, kid, you was great.

SOHOVIK

Next spot—the World Series.

WELCH

Shut the gate, nobody else in here.

GUARD

Nobody else in here.

158

VOICES

Who says so? etc.

GUARD

(*Holding them back*)

Mr. Welch says so.
(*The noise from the stands is cut off as if a door had been closed.*)

WELCH

One of you boys get Van Buren.

SOHOVIK

I'll get him.
(*Exits.*)

HENRY

(*Enters*)

Hey, they want us on television.
(*Boys exit in that direction,* SMOKEY *and* ROCKY *arm in arm, singing "Heart."* VAN BUREN *enters.*)

WELCH

I've shut the crowd out, Benny, and the reporters until I get this thing straight. Is Joe all right?

VAN BUREN

He's disappeared.

WELCH

He can't disappear.

159

VAN BUREN

I can't find him.

WELCH

Benny, it looked as if something happened to him right while he was running for that ball.

VAN BUREN

That's what I saw. He took off like a rabbit, then all of a sudden it looked like something hit him, he hobbled like he was lame, he was like a different man. Clumsy. There she goes I thought we'd blow it again. Then by God he made that last lunge and caught the ball. I tried to get to him to find out what was the matter, but the crowd got in the way. He ran into the club house and I haven't seen him since.

SMOKEY

(*Enters with* JOE's *pants in his hand*)
Benny—Joe's clothes are gone. We found his pants by the locker.

VAN BUREN

Come on.
(*They run out. There is a loud cheer from the team offstage. Blackout. In the darkness,* RUSS HODGES *can be heard, coming over the radio.*)

RADIO SPEECH: *Russ Hodges*

Neither Mr. Welch nor Benny Van Buren will affirm or deny the disappearance of Joe Hardy. However, many of the players admitted that from the moment he caught that ball and ran into the club house, none of them has seen him. *Where is he?*

Scene VI

MEG'S *house:* MEG *is lying on the sofa crying silently.* JOE BOYD *enters cautiously. She hears the front door close.*

MEG

Is that you, Sister? (*Getting no answer, she sits up, sees him and rises*) Joe!

JOE

I'm back.

MEG

Joe. (*Straightening her hair*) Joe, I'm a sight.

JOE

A wonderful sight.

MEG

Joe—oh, Joe! (*She rushes into his arms*) Where you been? (*Quickly changes her tone*) Oh no, no. I didn't mean that. I wasn't going to ask that.

JOE

Don't ask it.

MEG

I didn't mean to.

JOE

Don't ever ask it.

MEG

I won't. (*A pause. Then with finality*) You've been on a secret mission. (*Embrace*) But you're back. (*Overcome, she goes back to couch and sits.*)

JOE

If you'll have me.
(*He sits at her feet with head in her lap. She begins to rub his back.* APPLEGATE *appears from behind the sofa.*)

APPLEGATE

All right, Joe.
(JOE *looks up startled.*)

MEG

Is something the matter?

JOE

Say things to me.

APPLEGATE

We've had our little joke.

JOE

(*To* MEG. *Heads together, her arms around his neck*)
Things about us.

APPLEGATE	MEG
(*Talking*)	(*Singing, oblivious of* APPLE-
Listen, Joe, it was a mean	GATE's *presence*)
trick to turn you back. It was	A woman doesn't know
an impulse and I regret it.	what she has
But I'll make amends.	Until she loses it.

You can show up tomorrow. You can be Joe Hardy again. Win the World Series, be a hero.
> (*Comes around couch on hands and knees*)

I'm not really a bad fellow, Joe—I'm just emotional. I've forgiven Lola too. Look.
> (*Points to porch.* LOLA *enters on porch*)

She wants you back, boy—

LOLA

Joe—Joe—
> (APPLEGATE *whispers in* JOE'S *ears. Getting no response, he jumps up and signals* LOLA *to do something*)

Joe—Joe—
> (LOLA *shakes her head no.*)

APPLEGATE

(*Losing his temper*)
Listen to me, you wife-loving louse you belong to me.
> (APPLEGATE *jumps up and down.* LOLA *laughs at him. He*

When a woman has the love of a man
She abuses it
I didn't know what I had when I
Had my old love

I didn't know what I had 'til
I said goodbye, old love

Yes a woman doesn't know
What she has 'til it is
No longer around

MEG AND JOE

But the happy thought is
Whatever it is that's lost
May some day once again

163

rushes at her, and she
feigns innocence, then
he runs back)

You crook, you thief, you   Be
two-timing false-faced swin-
dler! You've robbed me,
you've robbed me!   Found!

Curtain